Path of the Mystic

Ai Gvhdi Waya

Chapters in this book
were previously printed in the
Sedona Journal of Emergence!

IBSN 0-929385-47-0

Published by:

P U B L I S H I N G
P.O. Box 1526, Sedona, AZ 86339
(800) 450-0985

Printed by

MI**SS**ION
PO**SS**IBLE
COMMERCIAL
PRINTING
P.O. Box 1495, Sedona, AZ 86339

Table of Contents

About the Author

Born in an Eastern Cherokee household, member of the Wolf Clan, with a father who was one-quarter blood, Ai Gvhdi Waya [pronounced *I-Jubdä-Y-ä*] was trained, beginning at the age of nine, in the medicine path. Although this medicine was never given a name, the closest description of it is *shamanism.*

Her life is devoted to healing Mother Earth and all her relations. She does this by being a practicing classical homeopath, a medical astrologer, creator of natural flower and gem essences, and by writing books to empower people to get in touch with their own unique being.

She is the author of *Soul Recovery and Extraction,* the shamanic process she was taught since childhood. Over the years she has trained a few hand-selected facilitators to carry on her work around the world with this process. She takes on no students, preferring instead that those who are interested trust their own inner guidance and get in touch with their inner teachers.

To communicate with Ai Gvhdi Waya:

Please visit her Internet website, The Medicine Garden at http://www.lyghtforce.com/athena. She has a mailing list of subscribers and is on-line every day teaching and sharing alternative-medicine information so that people can help themselves heal. All are welcome to subscribe. E-mail her at docbones@sedona.net or write: Blue Turtle Publishing, P.O. Box 2513, Cottonwood, AZ 86326.

COVER ART: *She Who Walks in Beauty*	Charles Frizzel, P.O. Box 738 Salida, CO 81201

Cover Design: Karen J. Holub

Introduction

"*P*ath of the Mystic." What does that mean? According to the dictionary, *mysticism* is a "doctrine that it is possible to achieve communion with God through contemplation." Another definition says, "Any doctrine that asserts the possibility of attaining an intuitive knowledge of spiritual truths through meditation."

I believe that how we live our daily life is our mystical path. We try to work from the heart chakra, that fulcrum between our lower three chakras and those above the heart. Without heart being involved, we will never truly make that quantum leap, that ascension, that transformation from chrysalis to butterfly. That means we must place our mind chatter, our logic, in a place of balance with our emotions, feelings and intuition, or inner knowing, in order to strike the harmony or balance in order to be prepared to make this conscious change from gross physical body into living, radiating spirit that glows from the inside of us outward – and extends into our everyday life in our everyday world.

How we live our life daily is the real testament of our spirit, which struggles to do the right thing to earn that vaunted transformation. As in no time in our human history have we been given the gift, the self-empowerment to blend our human self with our mystical, heart-centered self.

We are all mystics, whether we know it or not. Our spirit inevitably hungers for communion with God, Great Spirit, or whatever your belief system holds for you. My definition of a mystic comes from my Native American upbringing via my part Eastern Cherokee father. I was raised in a household of stories. My father never said, "Don't do this" or "Don't do that." Instead, if he saw me doing something that might hurt me or create pain because I didn't know any better yet, as a child, he'd tell me or the other siblings a story. And in the story were some seeds of truth mixed with experience.

Sometimes he told us stories about himself, his growing-up years, his years in the Navy during World War II, or stories that had been passed down through familial lineage. These stories had a beginning, middle and end. They weren't preachy, rather, instructive. It was up to me or my sibling to glean from the story what applied to us, or to a particular situation.

Even though I come from a line of medicine people via my father, the truth is that everyone is struggling to become a mystic – and is one – if they would allow themselves to be. It is simply a question of how awake or asleep one's spirit is; that is all. Mysticism belongs to all two-leggeds and four-leggeds, the Little People and the Winged Ones. There is a flow of life energy that binds us, flows through us and around us, that connects us to one another.

We become more conscious of this magical, mystical "flow," as I term it, the more we move from our lower three chakras into our heart. At this time on Mother Earth we are learning to do just that. It is an inner, mystical journey we must each take, on our own, without any outer teachers – only our own jaguar or wolf instinctive knowing – as our guide. To make this mystical journey into our heart so we can ascend to the next step in our spiritual evolution, we must make this adventure into our own unique one. No one's journey will be quite the same. The experiences walked through and hopefully learned from, will not be the same old thing for everyone.

Indeed, the path of the mystic is one of the most exciting journeys we take in a given lifetime – the exploration of our inner self. What lies within us? What jewels? What creativeness? What thoughts? Knowings? Just feeling my way through these questions inevitably excites me. An inner journey is truly one of raw, pure power in its more elemental form. Why? Because you have no guides, no outer teachers, just your own inner knowing, your ability to trust yourself, your instincts, about where you are flowing and going to reach your heart chakra to make that transformation.

From my training I was taught the only teacher was the one inside myself. I was not to rely on, believe in or do what other outer teachers did. Rather, to get into my flow, my heart. I had to move within myself to see who lived there – warts and all. Making the inner journey is like opening Pandora's Box – you just never know what one is going to find. Sometimes, it's pretty exciting. Other times, it's horribly disappointing or sometimes, terrorizing. Whatever we find is ours to own, keep and work through and either shed like the skin of a snake, or add to ourselves like an evolving clay sculpture that is taking on a refined shape – only it's done from the inside out.

What I am saying is that you are your own best teacher. At best, the stories in this book, which are about my life and its ups and downs, can serve as parables from which you might learn something that you can compare to your own life. Stories are always instructive – and at their best, can be used to reflect where you are now and, perhaps, where you want to be. If anything, these true accounts of my life are really about following my inner knowing and trusting myself to always move forward on that instinctual level.

Developing a trust of ourselves is the most important thing we can do. When we trust that little, urging voice inside us, in our heart, urging and coaxing us to do this or that, to go this way or that way – even though we're filled with fear and our head is screaming at us – if we can move through our fear, through the mind chatter and move in sync with that inner voice, then you have stepped onto your own mystical path.

Being a mystic isn't easy. It's challenging in every way. Saying you are a mystic is saying that you are on an inner journey deep into the subconscious well of yourself in search of your own, unique truth– whatever that might be. And walking a mystic's path means listening to inner teachers and guides; not outer ones. Once you get into your flow – and you will know that you are in it by the synchronicity of events that seem to keep popping up on an everyday basis – you will feel different. That does not mean you feel superior to anyone; but being in that mystical flow will give you a new level of self-confidence and self-esteem.

When you are in your flow, your life will work for you. When you're out of that mystical flow, you will encounter all kinds of walls, blockages and the inability to make things work – no matter whether it's in your personal life, your career or your goals and dreams.

I had three outer teachers in my Native American journey. First, there was my father. He gave me stories to live my life by and permission to live my own story and share it with whomever I chose. My second teacher, who wishes to remain anonymous, was a Western Cherokee medicine man. I call him Sam, although that's not his real name. He gave me a precious gift and one that I'd like to pass on to each of you. When I met him, he took one look at me and said: "Go home. Each day, meditate. Keep a journal. Do this for a year. At the end of that year, come back and see me."

I did. In that year I managed to meditate each day – and only missed about twenty days out of the year when I simply couldn't do it because of life's demands. In that year I "blew open" on a deep, deep internal level. Sam had knowingly guided me to place me on my inner, mystical path to my heart. I didn't know it at the time, but looking back on it, there's no question of his gift to me. As with all traditional Native American medicine people who are truly in touch with their personal power, Sam did not disempower me; rather, through his order for me to go home and claim myself, start my inner journey to true selfhood, he empowered me. I find few outer teachers today who are doing that for people who come to them seeking answers.

My third teacher, Oh Shinnah Fast Wolf, an Apache/Mohawk medicine woman, put me in touch with the Rock Nation and I allowed myself to move into my own genetic knowing of the Stone People, who opened up yet another world within me. She too, empowered me. She was a wonderful teacher, warts and all.

The real joke here is: We all have the answers, but we're looking in the wrong place. We defer and give our power away to other frail human beings, who are struggling just as much as we are — only they might not look like they are! And in doing so, we disempower our-selves in the process. Part of being a mystic on the path is learning discernment. That means that every person, situation and thing you encounter outside and inside yourself is your teacher. We need to learn what we're being taught. We need to listen — at the same time. We need to sift through what is being said and run it past our heart, our inner knowing, or voice. If it feels good and right to us, we can take it and make it ours. If it does not, we need to learn to trust what we know without being able to prove it, and release it because it's not a truth or piece of information that will serve us and empower us to remain on our own mystical path and process.

The parents in our lives are frail human beings who do their best to help us grow from newborn to adult. They probably weren't per-fect in their job as parents, but that didn't mean they didn't try their best for us. When moving on the mystical path one needs to learn from the environment we chose, as a spiritual being, while growing up. That does not mean we drag it around like "woundology" for the rest of our lives. To be a mystic means to learn from and through our parents — and then get on with life. Bless them, love them and honor them for what they gave each of us.

There is another "parent" in our life and from my Native American viewpoint, she is the most overlooked and underutilized. She is our Mother Earth — our true, real mother from which our heart is auto-matically connected with at birth. Unfortunately many people sever this umbilical cord with her for many different reasons. It is impor-tant to re-establish that connection if you are to be on a mystical path. She has always fed us, nurtured us and can support us in our goal to take our inner journey. To simply go and sit by a tree and meditate is doing it. Or finding a spot that seems particularly ener-getic and invigorating and positive to you is another way. Working with Mother Earth is a wonderful way to reconnect. It is the way I went. It's not the only way but one of many.

In the "old days" mystics who wanted to become mystical went to a monastery or into some deep, hidden place in the mountains away from everyday life in order to achieve enlightenment. Nowadays this process is available to each of us in our "real time" lives. We don't need to go to a monastery in the Himalayas to reach our enlighten-ment. No, we just need to take half an hour each day and devote ourselves to being quiet and listening to our inner voice – whether we do that in nature in concert with Mother Earth, in a room in our homes or wherever. The most important thing is to do it. Be disci-plined about it. It says that you feel worthy of your inner goal to step onto your mystical path.

I wish you an exciting, fulfilling inner journey into selfhood and transformation – the path of the mystic.

Our Own Best Teacher

During the past year, because I've been writing monthly articles for the *Sedona Journal of Emergence!*, I've received a number of letters. Some of the people who wrote wanted to experience soul recovery and extraction (SR/E). That was an easy request because I could refer them to any one of the facilitators mentioned in the back of the book I'd written on the topic.

Other letters were from people who wanted me to teach them my shamanistic methods. I told each person who wrote that I honored the old-fashioned method of being taught – from the inside out. I had no teacher of shamanism when I started this learning process. The method did not come to me out of the blue; rather, it was five years after I began to open up that I started to see the larger, overall pattern of what I was doing.

At all times I deferred to my inner guides, spiritual teachers who have advanced beyond human body form and who are known by many labels – angels, guardian angels, power animals, guides and so on. It was they who determined how fast I should learn the technique and how far I should go in putting what I had learned into actual practice. That was a five-year unfoldment process.

Since that time I have carefully chosen people to carry on the work. None of them came to me and asked me to teach them. Rather, the universe, in its infinite wisdom, placed in my path those people who were already shamans but didn't know it. I had the intelligence at those times (although sometimes I don't, believe me) to recognize why they were there and what they were doing in my life.

All my facilitators are friends as well as associates. I've known some of them for as long as sixteen years. I let time be the determiner, the final test, especially if I'm watching a possible shamanic candidate. No matter who the people are, over a period of time they will reveal their true selves, warts and all. By the same token, when I'm considering a potential facilitator, they get to know me, warts and all.

I have a real angst about women giving their power away to a teacher, be that teacher a woman or a man. Recently, a woman who had previously written called me. Bound and determined to track me down, she finally did. When I answered the phone, she told me she wanted me to be her teacher. "Judy" (not her real name) had been suckered in by another so-called (her words) shaman, a woman who had a correspondence course and all sorts of things available for the would-be shaman — at a price, of course. I told Judy that, first of all, I come from a strict Native American tradition in which the teacher never makes the students pay any money for what they receive. To do so, in my reality, is unconscionable.

After nine months with that woman, Judy discovered she was being duped and got angry enough to extract herself from the situation. I praised her for having the courage and strength to do that. Often people are taken for outrageous sums and don't wake up until years afterward.

Judy then asked me to take her on as a student. I said no. My policy is not to teach the world or anyone who writes or calls. I'm enough in touch with my universal flow to know when the Great Spirit puts a potential candidate in my path. As Judy continued to talk, it became obvious that she wanted to give her power away — again. But this time, to me.

I've seen too many women give their power away in too many other situations. I'm certainly not going to encourage it in my realm or in my life. I told Judy that if she wanted SR/E, she should contact my facilitators. I gave her their phone numbers to help her along on this path.

A couple of days later I received a phone call from one of my facilitators telling me Judy had called. She felt they had connected well. A few days after that I got a call from another facilitator whom Judy had called. He said that he had turned her down. The gist of these communications was that Judy was shopping around, trying to give her power away to someone. My people are carefully trained to recognize this sad situation and will, under no circumstances, take someone else's power, no matter how badly that person wants to give it away.

I had told Judy in the first phone call that if she were to be a shaman, she needed to get in touch with herself --not go to an outside teacher. She should learn to trust herself first. How many of us do, I wonder? How many of us have deferred automatically to someone who looked confident, poised and in control? I know I have, especially when I was younger. I'm older now, almost crone age, and I rarely give my power away to anyone any more.

Judy's dilemma is a common one, and my heart goes out to anyone in this situation. I have repeatedly said that our best teacher is inside ourselves, not outside. Even though Sam, my Cherokee medicine man teacher, was in my life for two years, he had nothing to do with my shamanic path or opening. All he did was open up what was genetically mine in the first place and help me to get back in touch with my Cherokee knowing. For that I'll always be grateful. But Sam was a human being, too. When I realized, on one trip out to California to visit him, that he was an alcoholic, it rocked my world. In fact, my world shattered, because I'd set Sam up as being better than I was in every way. Sam, to his credit, never took my power and never took advantage of me. For that I will always honor him. He was a human being caught in the terrible grip of alcoholism, but he didn't denigrate his relationship with me along the way. He did with another student, but that was not my path with him.

Sam was a wonderful teacher. He taught me by being human, warts and all. He gave me an eloquent lesson about how to conduct myself in the future, once I did decide to teach a few individuals my shamanic method of healing. My facilitators were my "training wheels" as a leader, and bless them, they put up with me. When you work with people, no matter at what level, whether casually or intensely, there has to be give and take. There has to be mutual respect and mutual teaching — teaching that goes both ways. I've always said people have been my best teachers.

So do you need a teacher in your life? Or do you really need to go within, to trust your own internal sense of knowing, that special place in your heart and gut that makes you the unique individual you are? Can you trust who you are? Do you know who you are? I find so many women who are out of touch with themselves and who they really are. It's easy for someone outside of ourselves to see us, but not as easy for us to see ourselves!

Do you find yourself automatically acquiescing to other people, no matter whether you know as much as or more than they do? Are there situations that you could handle but are afraid to try? Are you afraid to trust yourself? Do you always search for a human, outer teacher instead of trying an inner journey?

The greatest gift Sam gave me was my marching orders: Meditate daily for a year and keep a journal of what happens. I'd like to give this suggestion to anyone reading this article. How will we find out who we really are unless we become quiet and go within? How will we know what our special, sacred song is unless we grow quiet enough to hear it? What visions are awaiting us but can't come because we choose not to still our outer life enough to see and hear them?

So many people want to learn shamanism—it's a fad now. I'll be glad when it's over! Being a shaman is a lifelong work, and it's not for the weak or faint of heart. Shamanism is about dying — over and over again, in so many ways, on so many levels. If you like a life of continual chaos, change and transformation, then maybe you are shaman material. I still say that if you are to become one, it will happen. You need not spend thousands of dollars to learn what you already know.

You see, if you are to be a shaman, the kernel is already alive and growing within you. All you need to do is give it time, silence and commitment, and it will begin to grow within you. It is that simple. But then, I find that in this day and age, everyone wants to make things complex and tougher than they really are. Your answers—all of them—reside within yourself.

That is not to say that we don't run into daily teachers. We do. They are our co-workers, the person standing in the grocery line with you, the person pumping gas at the same time you are. Just sit and observe in a shopping mall, and you will find all the teachers you need—and then some!

Life isn't about searching for that teacher who will make things okay for you. It is irresponsible to give such a task to another human being. Some of you are here in this lifetime to learn that lesson, so you keep giving your power away to someone you see as stronger and more knowledgeable than yourself. Until you "get it," you will continue to move from one human teacher to another, always ending up angry and disillusioned. But who made the choice? You did, not the teacher. Who went looking for a teacher? You did.

We come here having chosen certain things we'd like to learn for our soul's development. We come here to pay back karma that is rightfully owed to others. I honor the path of the seeker, those of you looking for your ultimate teacher. It can be a very long, disappointing journey. I know, I run into you all the time. I was one myself when I was younger. I pray for you, pray that you find the inner light and beauty of yourself, which is more dazzling, more wondrous than the light and beauty of any human teacher outside yourselves.

What Is Shamanism?, Part 1

RECEIVING MEDICINE THE OLD-FASHIONED WAY

*B*ack in the "olden days" a medicine woman, or shamanness, would receive her medicine through face-to-face encounters with the animal itself. In North America, it wasn't uncommon for a medicine man or woman to send the student out to meet the animal with whom the student was to meld and become one. The whole idea was that an exchange be made on a spiritual level, with each party giving something to the other. That meant that if a student had had dreams about bears or if the teacher knew the student should acquire bear medicine, then the student was prepared and sent on her way to "call" a living bear to her to make the exchange. If the ceremony, the song(s) and the student's intent were there, the bear appeared. Of course, medicine people lost many of their students to the animal if the situation wasn't "right."

An old Navajo by the name of Coffee-Chili adopted my entire family when I was living on the Navajo reservation while growing up. He was like a wonderful old grizzled grandfather. The year before we moved onto the reservation, he'd been riding his scrawny horse out across the red-colored desert of New Mexico and had been struck by lightning during a fierce thunderstorm. The horse died instantly, and Coffee-Chili was struck deaf and dumb, no longer able to hear or speak. He'd never spoken a word of English anyway, so he signed in Indian sign language to my father, who was part Eastern Cherokee.

Coffee-Chili always told us stories with gestures, funny faces and noises or by play-acting the animal or thing he was trying to convey to us children. One time he told us that in order to heal the sick, the medicine person or shaman would first have to be bitten by a rattlesnake. If the person lived after this experience, she had then attained the right to utilize her ability to lift poisons from other people's bodies. I remembered that story as if someone had branded it on my mind. Now I know why.

At the age of nine I began my metaphysical training, which had been set up by my father. He wasn't a medicine man but he was a shaman; the abilities came naturally to him. Of his four children, he'd chosen me to carry on the shamanic tradition. I didn't know this at the time; I just did as I was told and put into practice what he showed me.

Later, I met a woman who was being taught by a Western Cherokee medicine man I'll call Sam. I met and liked him, but in the two-year period I knew him I was taught mostly secondhand by his favorite woman student. The best thing he did for me was to arrange crystal training under Oh Shinnah Fast Wolf, an Apache medicine woman, who he felt was the best crystal healer in North America.

The crystal healing proved to be a door that opened my genetic inheritance, knowledge and memory. Cherokees are the keepers of the crystals, and working with these wonderful rock teachers switched on a light within me that allowed me to learn shamanism from my own internal teachers.

Among Native American traditions, it is the teachers within a person that are most highly honored, not the teachers in physical bodies. Why? Because we are taught to honor ourselves and our feelings and to trust our intuition without question. This also develops a self-confidence that can never be taken away, because it was not given to a person by an outsider. By this stage in my life I was aware of some of my medicine teachers. In modern vernacular they are called power animals, which is a misnomer.

Originally, a power animal was supposed to mean a spirit guide in the guise of an animal/insect/reptile/plant body who possessed a "power." Power was meant to be another word for a skill or talent. Today I see it being abused and equated with power over someone or something, an ego trip, or all of the above. To avoid confusion, a medicine teacher is one who comes to a person from the realm of spirit and offers itself and its unique talents and skills to that person.

For example, a woman possessing owl medicine would be working on owl ways of walking or becoming. It could mean that the owl was teaching her to travel at night in her dreams, perhaps in a shamanic way, to fly to different worlds or dimensions, or to be able to tell truth from lies — to discern those who might lie to her as well as the lies she might tell herself. A person receiving a medicine teacher is expected to develop those special skills. All this time the medicine teacher is the guide, the knower, the teacher and the supporter of this person who wants to become owl.

Because we are all related and nothing is ever disconnected, separated or apart from anything else, regardless of the dimension, the Native Americans know that our friends, the ants, bees, snakes, winged ones and four-footed ones, approach us from time to time and offer their medicine and skills to each of us. Many people don't realize that if they see this animal (or insect, reptile and so on) three times, they should pay attention. For instance, if they see a coyote three times within a short period — say three weeks to a month — then this is coyote's way of offering her medicine to them.

What to do if this happens? Upon the third appearance, mentally or verbally tell the animal/insect/reptile that you accept his/her medicine and ask it to please come and teach you its skills and talents. Then go home and read up on this animal/insect/reptile. Find out its habits, nature and skills. See how these apply to you. Coyotes are known to be the trickster, the clown, and they possess a great sense of humor and the ability to laugh. Can you laugh? Did you know that laughter is a great healer? Or are you tricking yourself in some way? Or are you tricking others, either consciously or unconsciously?

Coyotes never go straight to a dead animal. No, they might circle for miles around the quarry before they ever get close enough to eat it. Perhaps you need to take time to learn to be more like a coyote in the way you approach business or your personal life. Do you just jump in without looking? A coyote never jumps on his quarry — he circles it, while he looks, watches, listens and waits — to make sure

it's safe to go pick up the quarry and eat it. Maybe you should follow his natural teaching and develop this skill.

JAGUAR MEDICINE PREDICTED

While developing my shamanic talents, I had acquired a number
of medicine teachers over the years. About five years ago some of my
teachers informed me that I would be moving into jaguar medicine.
I thought it was kind of odd at the time – after all, I lived in North
America, not South America, and the jaguar is distinctly a southern
cat. I shrugged and said that was fine, and never thought anymore
about it. Two years later my teachers again informed me that I
would receive jaguar medicine. I thought that I would receive it as I
did all the rest – through altered-state activity as a shamanness.

Shortly after that last subtle hint, I received an unexpected invitation to go to Sao Paulo, Brazil, and give several days of workshops
on crystal and gem healing. My host, a Brazilian, was an engineer
who was vastly interested in gemstones and crystals. While I was
thrilled with the prospect, in the back of my mind I thought, Aha, I'll
probably see a jaguar at a Sao Paulo zoo! Then I will receive the
medicine. I thought no more about it.

My host, whom I'll call Manuel, faxed me about three months later
to ask if I would like to go deep into the Amazon jungle outside of
Manaus, the old rubber city. He said there was a hotel in the middle of the jungle but that it had no electricity or running water. Were
we interested? You bet! We would have three days in the heart of
the Amazon Basin, and I wanted to commune with and honor the
spirits of that country with ceremony. I also wanted to see first hand
the destruction that was going on, as I'm very active in environmen-
tal issues.

The week spent in Sao Paulo was a complete success, but my
mind and heart were really on the three days we were to spend in
the jungle. We flew to Manaus, which sits on the banks of two
mighty rivers that merge to form the Amazon. We took an old wood-
en tugboat on a three-hour trip down the Amazon River. My host
had two young daughters, ages seven and ten, and I had given each
of them a tobacco bag so they could "gift" our relatives.

The captain of the tug told my host in Portuguese that there were
freshwater dolphins around but that we wouldn't be lucky enough
to see any. I told the girls to throw a handful of tobacco into the
Amazon as a gift and to ask the river spirit to invite the dolphins to

come to us so that we could honor them as well. Within fifteen minutes the first dolphin was sighted – large, gray and overwhelmingly beautiful. Within minutes dolphins were leaping all around us like excited children. Needless to say, the captain was surprised and was looking at me with the weirdest expression – one of wariness combined with curiosity and much respect. I smiled at him.

As we neared the channel where the hotel sat, the captain said that sometimes, only at night during a full Moon, one might see the very rare and almost-extinct pink dolphin. Manuel's children were fast to catch on and gave a second gift of tobacco to the river, asking specifically for a pink dolphin to appear. Within ten minutes, as we slowed to make the turn into the wide, still channel of muddy water, the first pink dolphin arced up and out of the water, not more than fifty feet away from the tug. This time the captain just about leaped out of the boat. The children screamed with glee, waving their hands and shouting to the pink dolphin who had also brought many of her cousins. We saw three or four pink dolphins from time to time as we slowly moved up the channel, which was completely covered with jungle on both sides.

The hotel consisted of a group of native grass huts sitting clustered together about a half mile from where the channel ended. We hiked in, carrying our luggage. It was hot and steamy, near dusk. The odors were all so different and yet familiar to me. By the time we arrived it was nearly dark, and as we were led to our hut with a flashlight, I had a premonition that a jaguar was present but was too tired to do anything about it.

Around 5 a.m. the next morning I awoke refreshed and vibrating with anticipation – over what, I didn't know. I woke my husband and we agreed to take an early morning exploratory hike. There was a small stream and a wooden bridge a quarter of a mile from the village. As we walked hand in hand down a hard-packed trail, the sky took on a surrealistic tone. The haze and fog hung in the tall, silent jungle trees and vines, the muted glow of Father Sun, not yet risen, tinged the semitranslucent fog. I felt as if I were in the "twilight zone" – as if I were indeed on one of my shamanic journeys to another dimension.

ENCOUNTER WITH THE JAGUAR

As we neared the small wooden bridge, I anchored to a halt. There, sitting in front of the bridge, was a full-grown male jaguar!

The night before, one of the men who worked at the village told us that the owner had found a baby jaguar a number of years ago, fed it, befriended it and then let it go. He said that from time to time the jaguar would come around if it hadn't found something to eat on its own, and the man would feed it.

I knew then, as I came to an abrupt realization, that my medicine teachers' foretelling of my coming into jaguar medicine was becoming a reality. The jaguar, who was lying down at the foot of the bridge, met my eyes and rose to a sitting position. I dropped my husband's hand and said, "He wants us to follow him." Then I took a step forward. The jaguar moved slowly and sleekly across the bridge. We were no more than a hundred feet behind him. At one point the jaguar stopped, turned and looked back to see if we were coming and then continued across the bridge.

My heart was pounding – I was thrilled and scared at the same time. My husband wasn't so sure it was a good idea. After all, the jaguar was wild, not tame. The jaguar moved off the bridge, turned right and went down a muddy bank to a small oval of lush green grass that lay next to the ribbon of stream. I smiled, breathless.

"Let's go down! He won't hurt us," I said and leaped off the bridge, sliding down the dry bank. The jaguar waited until we were both there, then moved to the edge of the bank. He looked at us and then at the water. At that moment, I received the impression he wanted to get into the stream and have us sprinkle him with water. I told my husband this message and he gave me a rolled-eyes response. Eagerly, I moved within a few feet of the jaguar. The cat turned and stepped daintily into the crystal clear water and lay down in it. The water was barely a foot in depth, and I knelt at the edge and cupped water across his yellow- and black-spotted back. My husband came closer, convinced that it was safe. The cat hadn't snarled, shown his teeth or made any move that looked threatening. We both knelt there, sluicing cool water across the jaguar's back for at least ten minutes.

I was in ecstasy over what was happening, a joy flooding me that was so keen that it was like an ache. I remembered Coffee-Chili's story about getting medicine the old-fashioned way – with a live animal, up-front and close. I recognized the dangers too, for I knew this jaguar was not tame in the least. As we got to our feet, the jaguar moved languidly out of the water and came to sit at our feet in the grass to lick himself off. At that point I begged my husband to go get the camera — which was back at the hut — so we could have a picture of this. My students would believe my story but I wanted a photo to back it up. After all, how many times would people nowadays receive their medicine in physical reality?

The jaguar and I were alone. I moved about ten feet away from the jaguar, and hunkered down in a crouched position, facing him. At that point, I felt the need to sing him my personal song, and I did. There was a surreal sensation about this time alone with him, but being a shamanness, it didn't bother me. I remained focused on what I wanted to do, which was to honor him by singing him my song. The cat continued to lick his paws as I sang. The instant I stopped singing, his head snapped up and his ears sheared forward.

I froze. The jaguar's eyes, once huge black pupils set in a thin crescent of gold, suddenly went to mere black pinpoints upon a blazing yellow background. I felt myself being forcefully pulled out of my physical body, my astral form crashing into and merging with the jaguar's body. I remained frozen, completely alert and awake to the fact that I was now inside the jaguar's body! I felt him, his strong musculature and all his feelings — which were powerful! It was an incredible moment. Then I knew that, at all costs, I had to get back into my own body.

All of the years of training, all of the times I practiced staying focused, were called upon in an effort to release myself from the jaguar's power. I pulled out of the cat, flying those ten feet back into my own body knowing without a doubt that he would leap on me and kill me. When one's astral body is out of the physical body, one cannot move a muscle; one is literally frozen to the spot, or collapses unable to move.

As I slammed back into my body, I rose in one simultaneous motion, jumped up, turned around in midair and hit that dirt bank at a dead run. Just as I scrambled to the top of the bank, I jerked a look across my shoulder. The jaguar was midleap and landed exactly where I'd been frozen milliseconds before! With a cry, I ran across the wooden bridge and up the hill as fast as my adrenaline could take me. When I got to the top of the hill, I met my husband. In a panic, I looked back. The jaguar had not followed me. Instead, he was standing in the grassy area, looking at me and switching his tail back and forth.

PHOTO OPPORTUNITY

Gasping for breath, my heart slamming into my ribs, I told my husband what had happened. He wanted to leave that moment, but I begged him to come back down to the bridge with me. I had to get a photo of that jaguar! I was very frightened of going back because now I could feel the jaguar as if I were still inside of him — each emotion, each frustration and anger. I realized as we approached the bridge that the age-old way of trading medicine between a human and animal had taken place.

I mentally told the jaguar what I wanted. He was pacing angrily back and forth on the grass, looking at me, his ears pinned back. He was pissed, to say the least. But I felt his respect for me, too. I took advantage of it. I told my husband to get far enough away to take a photo of me leaning down to touch the jaguar. I wasn't at all sure if the jaguar would leap up and bite me as I leaned precariously over the bridge. Perhaps he would bite my hand, savage my arm or completely haul me off and kill me.

The jaguar came over to me as I leaned down and extended my hand toward him. He lay down, switching his tail. Good! He couldn't jump me while he was lying down. As I quickly leaned over, I saw him start to get up. Without hesitation I touched his broad, sleek skull, turned to face the camera and smiled. My husband took the photo and instantly I jerked my hand back and climbed back onto the bridge. I thanked the jaguar and quickly walked away, looking over my shoulder from time to time. The jaguar lay back down in the grass beneath the shade of a tree next to the stream.

Back at the huts, I excitedly shared with Manuel what had happened. He just gave me an incredulous look and shook his head. Here's what he told me: Jaguars are known to be powerful spirit beings who have the capacity to freeze their quarry into immobility with a hypnotic look. Once the jaguar has frozen his quarry, he then leaps upon it and kills it.

Now I knew from firsthand experience how a jaguar accomplishes such a feat — and I lived to tell about it! Further, Manuel told me that in Central and South America jaguar medicine is considered to be the most powerful and the most sought-after. He didn't say why; that was for me to discover on my own. However, many medicine men have trained their students for years to come face to face with a jaguar, sing their song to it and then exchange spirits. Unfortunately, Manuel told me sadly, most of the students ended up either dead or so badly mauled that they remained crippled for the rest of their lives. Amazed by his facts, I felt not only blessed but lucky to be alive.

That trading of spirits happened two years ago, and I can honestly say my life hasn't been the same since. The jaguar now accompanies me in altered states whenever I work in someone's behalf. But I'm also discovering that jaguar medicine has a powerful connection to femaleness and feminine consciousness. I understand from Manuel that there is a jaguar cult and/or society in Central America, so who knows? Maybe someday, if it is meant to be, I'll meet others who have faced the jaguar and lived to tell about it.

What Is Shamanism?, Part 2

DEALING WITH THE DYING AND DEATH EXPERIENCE

*M*y family was raised within the tradition of shamanism. This is not to say we know everything there is to know about shamanism, for it varies from country to country and depends upon an individual's spiritual training and religious beliefs as well as one's genetic and cultural background.

It's true that we service those who are living, but equally true that in no other field with which I've been acquainted within the metaphysical disciplines do dying and death become such a central focal point as in shamanism. As we deal with those who are living, we also deal with those who are dying or dead.

I've always said that a *shaman* (I will use this term to denote either a female or male practicing or facilitating in the shamanistic mode) was nothing more than a bird dog retrieving pieces that have split off from someone's spirit, or a glorified message carrier. There's much truth to this, and it keeps my work in perspective for me. Further, the spiritual guardians from the unseen worlds work through us, so, we're little more than a conduit or empty tube for them to reach through to help another. And really, many times we stand by and watch! That keeps our egos in line and discourages the swelled-head syndrome.

GOING OVER THE RAINBOW BRIDGE

One of the greatest and most humbling parts that a shaman plays in the drama called life is helping another person pass over to the other dimensions. Because of my Eastern Cherokee training I call this transition "going over the rainbow bridge." It's a lovely way to envision a soul slipping peacefully from the body and moving up and over those unearthly, scintillating colors of the rainbow to reach the Other Side. From my shaman's perspective, I've always referred to this dimension as the "light world" because it is filled with such brilliant white light. For Christians, it is heaven. For others, it is nirvana and so on.

When I began my training in shamanism I had no idea that I was to help the dying move more quickly to the Other Side, or that shamans dealt with the spirits who have died but remain trapped here for various reasons. As the years went by my spirit guides opened my eyes to a broader format of what a shaman's responsibilities entail. When they felt I was ready, they positioned me to help a young man who was dying of AIDS.

HELPING THE RELEASE

I had received a call from the young man's lover, Alex (not his real name), to come to the hospital; he'd specifically asked for me by name. When I asked how he knew of me, he told me that John (not his real name) had read a book I'd written. I agreed to go. Arriving at the hospital, I met John's grief-stricken family. Alex was the most coherent of anyone, so I asked him what was needed from me.

Alex pulled me aside and told me that John knew it was time to go and wanted to be released. I nodded and asked to see John. Those who have already been touched by the AIDS epidemic know, that in a hospital they post all kinds of warnings and regulations on AIDS patients' doors, such as suiting up in a gown and a surgical mask. I asked the family if they wanted to go in, but John's deterioration was too much for them to bear, so Alex and I went in to see him —without gowns or masks.

John lay in bed and I was surprised at how good he looked under the circumstances. Normally, AIDS causes a person to be little more than skin and bone before they die, but not John. He was very healthy-looking, his skin clear and his youthfulness so apparent. I could understand why his family found it so hard to stay in the room with him, since he didn't look ready to die.

As I stood just inside the door, I noticed two eight-foot-tall light-beings standing in the corner of John's room. I asked Alex if he could see them, but he said no. What he did say was that John had told him that his friends were there and would often point to the same corner I was pointing to. Sometimes when John was semiconscious, he would speak to them directly and hold conversations with those beings. I put my hand up, in a gesture asking Alex to remain silent while I contacted them telepathically.

I found out that these lightbeings were John's guardians, who were responsible for taking him into the light once he was ready to go. From a Christian perspective they would probably be considered guardian angels. I asked permission from them to be with John and they approved. These guardians appeared as long, slender ovals of brilliant white light tinged with gold. I didn't see faces or shapes, just their very loving, serene spirit and energy. I asked them if I could in some way help John. They said yes.

John was dozing lightly, but when Alex tenderly touched his shoulder, his eyes flew open. I was standing at the foot of the bed and smiled at John as he came awake. Almost instantly he lifted his hand and croaked, "You came!"

I moved to the other side of the bed and grasped John's outstretched hand. "Alex called me, John. How are you doing?"

He grimaced and swallowed with some effort. Alex placed his arm beneath John's shoulders, lifted him slightly and gave him a sip of water. John thanked him, his voice soft and somewhat slurred. I found out that John was on a considerable amount of drugs and that he was only semilucid from time to time. In this moment he was extremely lucid, focused and in his body as he looked up at me.

"I want to go," he said. "It's time. I know you can help me."

I squeezed his hand a bit more and said, "I'll take a journey into an altered state and see if your chief guide will give me permission to help you, John. If I get the go-ahead, your guide will instruct me how to help you. Have you been able to say good-bye to everyone you want to?"

With tears in his eyes John looked at Alex. "I have." And then he closed his eyes and fell immediately into a deep slumber.

Alex issued a sigh and looked over at me. "He's finally asleep. That's good. He's been so restless for days, going in and out of consciousness."

I told Alex I would go home and do a journey on John's behalf and that I would call him at the hospital when I was done to give him and John's family a report. Alex gratefully nodded and I left.

In an altered state produced by my mother's drum beating, I went to my chief guide and asked her permission to help John. She approved and I went to John's hospital room. I saw Alex sitting at his bedside as he slept, John's hand in his own. I was deeply touched by Alex's care for him in these final days of his life.

GETTING ALL THE PIECES BACK

John's astral self came over to me. His arms were filled with symbolic pieces of spirit that he'd taken from others over his lifetime. He asked me to please give these pieces back to their rightful owners. I took them and visited six different people, blowing the pieces into them individually. When I was done, I came back. John was eagerly waiting for me.

"You've got to get my pieces back now. I can't leave my physical body until you've got them all back."

I found ten pieces of John that had been taken by others over his thirty years of life and brought them back to him. After I'd given them back, he smiled and hugged me.

"Thanks! Now I can go!" He was like an excited child who was about to embark on a wonderful journey that had a positive and good ending. I turned to his two guardians. "How long does he have to live now? I'd like to tell his family, if you don't mind."

"Two and one-half days," one of them answered telepathically.

After thanking them and my spirit guides, who had worked so hard on John's behalf, I left. Exactly two and a half days later John died peacefully with his family at his bedside. Knowing in advance when he would leave helped everyone concerned.

I found out from the guardians that people often transit, or die, without having given back pieces of spirit they've taken from others or without ever receiving back pieces that belong to them. When this happens, the person's spirit cannot move into the light world.

WAITING IN LIMBO FOR LOST PIECES

I know that this is true because when I've journeyed for people, I've been sent to just below the light world where I see, hanging there like bulbs on a Christmas tree, hundreds of thousands of spirits of those who have died, just below the glow of white light, but unable to enter. They hang there in limbo until pieces of spirit are given back or until they surrender the pieces they have of others.

Now, the people who need these pieces back might be either dead or alive. The soul hanging in limbo, awaiting the return of its own pieces might wait a long time – perhaps lifetimes! Meanwhile, the spirit of a deceased person might hang there just below the light, waiting for years for the exchanges to be made, or else continue to wander aimlessly between the "real world" (our third-dimensional reality) and the "dark world" (a dimension found within Mother Earth). They might choose to stay with their family or loved ones and just hang around. If they had drug addictions, killed themselves or were in some way traumatized in death by means of a brutal accident, a murder or some other kind of violent state, they will be found in the dark world. This is not the Christian hell, either. There is much beauty and goodness to be found in the dark world, just as there is in the real world.

These are not necessarily unhappy places for the departed spirit who still carries the baggage of others or is not whole. The saddest are the suicides or violent deaths. They are still caught up in the terror or despondency of their last moments before taking of their life. The good news is that if the shaman has permission to help them, they can be released. One of my happiest journeys is releasing a spirit and helping it zoom into the light world where it is lovingly greeted by relatives or dear friends. I can't begin to share with you the joy I feel when this happens. I always come out of the journey with tears streaming down my face – tears of joy! Another soul has been released and now can begin to evolve once more on its chosen path of learning.

Souls that are "stuck" in either of the two other dimensions described cannot continue their evolutionary progress until such time as they give back the pieces that don't belong to them or retrieve lost pieces taken from them by others. They will spend lifetime after lifetime trying to make the trade with those from whom they have taken; hence, repetitive karmic situations are experienced in however many lifetimes it takes until the soul learns that it is not right to take something from another soul.

When souls have their parts taken by other people they too will karmically continue lifetime after lifetime until those who have stolen them give the pieces back. This is the way we learn, unfortunately. It's not fun, it's not fast and usually it's quite painful.

With shamanic intervention (providing the approval is given by the chief guide), pieces can be given back or gotten back for the person who is dying. Then, instead of hanging around for an indeterminate amount of time, she or he can go straight to the light upon leaving the body. I can't think of a finer gift to a loved one than to have a shaman journey for them as they lay dying. It's a final gift of love.

Recently, the mother of one of my associates lay dying. She called and asked if I would journey on her behalf, because emotionally she just wasn't strong enough to do it herself. I said I would, understanding completely.

When I entered Thelma's (not her real name) hospital room, she jumped out of her physical body and came to greet me. I didn't even get to speak to the two guardians who stood there patiently waiting. She threw me several symbolic pieces that needed to be given back and waved me vigorously away with her hands, saying, "Hurry!"

THE ∫HΛFT OF WHITE LIGHT

After giving back the pieces, she insisted I get her pieces back. I noticed that a brilliant shaft of white light shone down upon the hospital bed where her physical body lay. It was as if someone were shining a very bright flashlight into the room through the ceiling above the bed. When a person is ready to go, I've found that this shaft of light shimmers around and through them. In near-death experiences this is what people refer to as a tunnel of light.

Coming back a second time, Thelma grabbed my arm, choking on tears, and told me to tell her daughter how much she loved her and how she hated to leave her. I smiled and gripped her hand and said, "Yes, but she's a shamanness and can come and visit you in the light world any time she wants."

Thelma's face lit up with such surprise and gratitude that I felt tears in my eyes.

"Oh! That's right! That's right, she can!" With that, she slipped back into her physical body. I turned and saw the guardians moving silently toward me. I stepped out of the way and watched a very beautiful thing occur. As they went into this shaft of light, I saw them both extend a hand to Thelma, who came easily out of her physical shell. They drew her astral form out of the rear neck region, and the cord from it was still attached to her physical body at the heart chakra. A soul needs time to adjust to the energy of the light, and once it has, it will tell the guardians that it's ready to leave. At that time the cord between the astral form and the physical form disintegrates and the guardians gently lift the spirit of the person upward into the tunnel of light.

The three of them stood there together, Thelma flanked by her loving guardians. I realized they were allowing her to adjust to the tunnel of light and the new energy.

I asked the guardians how long it would be before she would leave and they said three days. I thanked them and left.

Shortly afterward I called the hospital where my associate was awaiting my call. I described all the pieces Thelma had given me and she verified all of them and the people they had gone to. My associate was grateful for the intervention and the great peace of mind she felt, knowing that in three days her mother would leave peacefully, without struggle or regret.

Three days later — to the hour — Thelma left her physical body and went over the rainbow bridge to the light world.

If one can see the aura, it is always gray-colored as death approaches, even months before the actual death. As one begins to go through the dying process, each of the auric fields begins to deteriorate and then dissolve, starting with the outside field and moving inward. As more fields disintegrate over a period of time, the person is able to free him/herself from most earthly concerns and turn the last of his/her consciousness upon leaving. The last field to leave is the etheric body, which is a tight-fitting, weblike field that encloses the physical shell much like a form-fitting glove. The etheric, when looked at closely, appears like cross-hatching, with fine, thin lines of energy criss-crossing one another like a fine weaving.

The shaft of light becomes even more powerful, more illuminating and glowing, as the guardians prepare to pull the astral form out of the physical body while the etheric body finally dissolves. The astral body is our emotional body, which holds all our hopes, dreams and fears. This is why some people are afraid to die up to the last moment — the fear within their astral form is still dragging out the process. A shaman can journey to help the person come to terms with what is happening. Very frequently a sensitive, gentle and reassuring talk with the person is all that's needed.

Our spirit, the part of our soul that is contained in the astral body, leaves the physical shell behind and moves upward toward the powerful shaft of light with the loving guardians. At a certain point the astral body dissolves and is shed, and the person can once again become a being of light.

SHAMANIC DUTIES

A shaman can play a vital role in the death process. She or he can talk to the guardians nearby when death is near. Over the years I have learned that if the guardians are in the corner of the room, the person has roughly five days to live. If they are halfway to the bed, three days. If they are next to the bed, death will be within 24 hours. Being able to tell the family when the person is going to transit is itself a huge gift. Further, a shaman can transmit messages back to the family of the one who is dying, just as I gave my associate the last message from her mother. This made all the difference in the world to her in handling her mother's death.

A shaman can quicken death so that the person suffers less and the family is released from that helpless, grieving mode. A shaman doesn't cause the death, but rather relieves the dying person of burdens he no longer wishes to carry, pieces she chooses to return before dying in order to balance the scales of karma. Once relieved of these burdens, the soul can move through the experience quickly and cleanly, allowing the family to suffer less.

Becoming a shaman means to expect a near-death experience — a chronic disease, an auto accident or some other traumatic incident. Some shamans experience numerous brushes with death or go into an actual near-death experience. Why? Because, as I have discovered in my own shamanic journey, we deal with the dead and dying fifty percent of the time. The other half of the time we are dealing with the living and their individual problems and traumas. Shamans cannot be afraid of death if they are going to service the dying or dead. Such a fear would stop us from being of value to those who seek our help.

There are two things I love doing most in this world: attending the birthing of a baby and attending someone who is dying. Amazingly, there is no difference. The same guardian lightbeings are in the room and the same powerful shaft or tunnel of light is there. In both instances there is such joy — whether about entering the body to begin life, or about leaving the body a final time. At many births and deaths I have heard chanting or singing or beautiful, cosmic music from the other dimensions. I wish everyone could see and experience what a shaman feels when someone transits. If you did, you'd never be afraid of death but would welcome it like an old, loyal friend. Further, there would be a party to celebrate a person's passing, because where they're going is a whole lot better than what we cope with here!

Grief would be less harsh and deep if people could absorb the beauty of dying, for they would experience the joy on the face of the person who is leaving. Death is only another birth — into another dimensional reality. The only grief left to feel is loneliness, and that can heal only with time. In many cases, when I've been contacted by a spouse left behind, I've had to exchange pieces between that person and the spouse who has died. At the last moment the remaining spouse might unconsciously take a piece of the loved one, not wanting them to die. Incomplete, the spirit who has died can't continue on. The spouse must surrender that part and unconsciously or consciously give it back.

In cases where the spouse grieves for more than three years, it is an indication that she or he still has a large piece of the deceased person's spirit. A shaman can journey and make the exchange, thereby releasing both parties so that they can get on with their individual paths.

Another phenomenon that occurs is when a husband dies and leaves his wife behind. He might have given back all pieces and collected all his own pieces, but still he remains with his wife, a spirit living in the house, or perhaps in the orchard or garden. Shamans can intervene in these cases; usually it's the deceased who is worried about the one left behind. I've talked to many spirits caught in this trap and have been able to reason with them and persuade them to leave for the light world. When they realize the spouse is really doing fine, they are relieved and go on.

A deceased spirit might have been tragically murdered or died a sudden death in some violent, unexpected way. It will hang around the area where the death occurred, still in psychic shock from the incident. A shaman can journey to this spirit, tell it what happened and gently, with love, lead it through the rest of the death process so it can go with its light guardians. As a spirit, we have choice. If we don't want to leave, for whatever reason, no one will force us to leave, for that is a part of our karmic experience.

SPIRITS CAN CHOOSE TO STAY

One time when we were living in the house in Oregon, my father had to talk to a spirit who loved his fruit orchard so much that when he died, he stayed within the area, not wanting to leave it because he felt he couldn't.

All of us kids picked night crawlers every night in the orchard after doing our homework to make money for books and clothing, because we were very poor. At first I sensed a spirit present as I was crawling around on my hands and knees in the mud. My brother, Gary, heard, as I did, his footsteps in the mud following us around in the orchard for hours. This finally got to us and we told our father. He said he'd talk to the spirit and see what could be done. The next morning, our father said he'd found out that it was the old man who had planted the orchard and lovingly tended it for forty years before he died. My father was able to help him leave after he explained that we would take care of his orchard as well as he did. Satisfied, the old man's spirit went on to the light world.

Another side of shamanism that's scary for many people is dealing with violent spirits who have such hatred, anger or some other negative emotion that they hurt humans. I remember one case when I was asked to come to a farm. The couple told me that each night in their attic there would be stomping sounds and things thrown about. Near dawn the sounds would stop. They asked me to find out what was going on.

On my journey I found a malevolent spirit in the two-story barn outside the house. He'd committed suicide after raping a neighbor's daughter in the cow pen. The man's spirit was distraught and angry, and he told me he didn't want anyone living in his house. I gently explained things to him and offered my help, doing quite a sales job convincing him to move on. Gradually the spirit came around and I was able to relieve him of many burdens and move him into the light world. After that experience the farm couple no longer heard sounds or experienced items being thrown around in the attic.

While at a conference in Georgia, Donna (not her real name) came over to me, very upset. She said it was ice cold in her hotel room and that she'd had nightmares about some kind of violence all night. She asked me to check it out, so I journeyed to the room. Sure enough, a spirit of a man who'd committed suicide by jumping out the window of that room was still there. It was easy to help this spirit; he moved on without a fuss.

A shaman intervenes — with permission — in many different ways and performs many different functions. It's our hope that by revealing the shaman's realm, you'll have a better sense of how we can help others. Life is as beautiful as death. We should not fear one and celebrate the other. Indeed, both are celebratory occasions because of the intense love that surrounds these two major events in each of our lives.

Sweat Lodge

*T*he sweat lodge is as old as woman and man on the face of Mother Earth. No Native American nation owns it, for it is practiced worldwide. Despite varying traditions, there is one common tie that binds each "sweating" and sweat lodge to all the others: it is a sacred place where one goes to cleanse one's spirit.

I spent a month and a half at the Rosebud Lakota Reservation with friend Patty Thomas, a Santee Sioux shamanness in her midforties. Patty was a sweat-lodge leader, but before my arrival I hadn't been aware of this aspect of her many talents.

My Western Cherokee teacher had warned me to always be discerning and careful about who I shared a sweat lodge with. As a result, even though I had invitations to participate in them, I never did. All the invitations had come from males running a "mixed" sweat (composed of men and women). I had no problem with men and women gathering for a sweat, because I believe in a balance of energies, but I had trouble with the sweat-lodge leader's energy or reason for holding the sweat. I had asked an acquaintance of mine who had the experience of building one hundred sweat lodges to help me make one on the land we steward. It took about half a day with sixteen people working like happy children. When it was done, we had a sixteen-person sweat lodge covered with opaque black plastic.

The first sweat performed in the lodge was led by my male companion with his drum and eagle-bone whistle (he's a six-time Sun Dancer). Fourteen of my associates flew in from around the country. The atmosphere of the group—trusted associates I'd known over the years—was right, and we had an incredible sweat-lodge experience.

Nine months later I met Patty Thomas on the reservation, where conducted daily or every-other-day sweat lodges for women only. I liked her and her energy. She was a short, stout Lakota woman with dancing brown eyes and thick, curly black hair. The day after I arrived at her place she invited me to come down and sweat with her and two of her friends.

EXPECT NOTHING, RECEIVE EVERYTHING

This first sweat had been a "cool" sweat. Having no idea what to expect at Patty's sweat, I recalled a great Cherokee saying: "Expect nothing, receive everything." I kept an open heart and mind about this coming experience. There were six Lakota women in the sweat —I was the only white woman present. They had much more sweat experience than I had. Fortunately, I had the good sense to wear my long cotton robe with long sleeves and take a towel.

We waited outside the sweat lodge while Patty filled her pipe inside, and the fire tender got the heated rocks ready to place inside. When Patty raised her hand, the women became silent and walked in a clockwise circle to the entrance. As each one got down on her hands and knees to move through the doorway, she murmured, "Mitakuye Oyasin." That is Lakota for "We are all related." Being the last one in, I sat opposite Patty, closest to the door.

Fresh, sweet-smelling sage was passed in a clockwise circle to each sister, and we rubbed it briskly on our arms, hands, necks and faces. One sprig was placed behind the right ear to show the spirits that our reasons for being present at the sweat were filled with heart and integrity.

Seven glowing-red rocks were placed one at a time in the pit in the center of the sweat lodge. Patty greeted each one with "Hau kola" ("Hello friend") and touched it with the stem of her pipe. Coletta, one of Patty's sweat sisters, placed a pinch of sacred herbs on each of the seven rocks. I sat there feeling the heat rise and was already beginning to sweat. Looking around, I noticed that no one else was sweating. Knowing I was the "baby" of the group, I had previously told Patty that I'd been in only one other sweat. She had nodded and smiled, saying nothing.

The lodge's flap was placed down by the fire tender and the warm, heated darkness engulfed me. I was vibrantly aware of the heady aroma of cedar and sage that surrounded us. The rocks glowed red from the pit, and in them I could see faces, both human and animal. The feeling in the sweat was one of profound unity, a solidarity I'd never before encountered. I liked the feeling, realizing that it was because we were all women—a strange but comforting feeling – and smiled in the darkness, closed my eyes and knew that never in my life could I be at a more appropriate place.

The bucket used to hold the water was huge. Several sprigs of fresh sage were captured beneath the handle and a wooden ladle floated in the water. Patty had told us that all the water had to be used in the sweat; we couldn't leave until the pail was empty. I began to realize dimly what that meant.

DEDICATION TO WHITE BUFFALO CALF WOMAN

Patty began to sing a song to White Buffalo Calf Woman, to whom she always dedicated the first round of the sweat. As she sang, she ladled water onto the stones. Hissing steam mingled with her clear, crystalline voice. Immediately I was hit with a wall of hot steam as it rolled down the sides of the sweat lodge, causing me to automatically lean forward toward the pit. Gasping, I couldn't breathe until I pulled the towel over my head and held the fabric against my nose. Mouth hanging open, I tried to switch my focus from my own shock and discomfort to something higher, more profound and sacred. Patty said before the flap was closed that if anyone felt like leaving because of the heat, she should think of someone far worse off. This would help her to endure.

After singing the four-directions song, Patty continued to ladle water into the pit. I felt like a scalded lobster thrown into a pot of boiling water. Fighting my own panic and sense of humiliation because I couldn't focus above my physical problems, I lay down on the floor. Instantly, there was some relief. Because heat and steam rise, cooler air is always at ground level.

Feeling slightly better, I knew that under no circumstance was I going to yell "Mitakuye oyasin" and scamper out the door of the sweat lodge. I knew Indians respect only one thing: courage. They disdain cowardice. I had to spend a month and a half with Patty and I wasn't about to start out my tenure with her by leaving the sweat. At that moment I made the internal decision to stay—no matter what happened.

PRAYER ALLEVIATEſ DIſCOMFORT

After the fourth song the flap was raised. I propped myself up a little and turned my head toward the opening, sucking in the cooling air. Water ran off me in rivulets. I was amazed, because I usually never sweat even under the most dire circumstances. Seven more stones were brought in and the flap was put down once again. In the second round, after three songs the prayer round began. Totaled by the burning heat, I couldn't think two thoughts coherently, much less speak. The heat was so oppressive and the steam so thick that I prayed only for the strength to remain.

When it was my turn to pray I sat up, head bowed, towel against my mouth and spoke. The words and feelings came pouring out of me, raw, unprepared, but gut-wrenchingly honest. I prayed for those I love, I prayed for my real mother, the Earth, who desperately needs healing, and I prayed for many who were sick and ailing. As I prayed out loud I noticed that all my physical discomfort left me. I felt as if I were floating, a miracle in itself.

The second round was the hottest and the longest. Some prayers lasted (I swear) 15 minutes. They were profound, from the heart and spoken with reverence. Surely the white part of me was wishing the prayer-speakers would hurry their prayers, but my Cherokee side understood and applauded the slow deliberatation of those sincere prayers. By the time the flap was opened, I felt like a well-done lobster. A river of water was cascaded off my hands and fingers and down my face.

My mouth was cotton-ball dry. To my great delight, Patty took a ladle of water and passed it around to each of us. Never had cooling water tasted so good. I wondered if I was going to dehydrate by the time I finished the sweat. I stole a look around at the Lakota women and they looked marvelously relaxed, peacefulness mirrored in their features. I didn't feel relaxed because I was worried I wouldn't be able to complete the next two rounds without crying out and leaving.

Seven more stones were added and the flap was dropped for the third round. It became hotter yet. I found solace in the fragrant earth pressed against my cheek and nostrils. Steam found me and I struggled with every bit of inner strength to lift myself beyond my physical misery. As I struggled, Patty's strong, clear voice rolled through the darkness, and I realized I had to surrender. Temporarily I forgot what my Apache teacher once told me: "The only thing we surrender to is a power higher than ourselves."

These words flowed through me like a powerful river of revelation and I understood that I had to surrender my burning flesh, my dehydrating body, to the Great Spirit and to my Earth Mother who held me as long as I lay upon her. Within seconds the heat and steam seemed muted and less tangible. I was floating somewhere in the darkness, feeling light and joyful. The throbbing of a heartbeat seemed to emanate from around me.

Disappointment came as the flap was raised. I sat up, blinking like someone returning from a very deep, restful sleep. The pipe was lit and Patty passed it to all of us. Our prayers were lifted to Father Sky and to the Great Spirit through curls of thick white smoke.

SURRENDERING TO A HIGHER POWER

Seven more stones were added for the fourth and last round. The flap was closed. When my focus strayed to my physical form, I was in trouble, but because I had surrendered to a power higher than myself, I lay down upon my Earth Mother and allowed Patty's Lakota songs to take me to that sacred place in the darkness once again. The heat didn't seem as intense and the steam relaxed its hold on my breathing.

When the flap was lifted, each woman crawled out in a clockwise circle and said, "Mitakuye oyasin," as she left. I was so dizzy that although I murmured the Lakota words, I kept crawling after I had emerged. My arms and legs trembled, and I knew I was close to dehydration. The cooling midafternoon air felt like air conditioning, and revived me slightly, still on all fours. I had to get up. I couldn't show any more weakness than I already had in front of these strong, wonderful women.

As I pushed myself to my feet, my knees became rubbery. I staggered forward and caught a branch of a nearby tree. Tunney came over and helped me to a chair. Someone else shoved a glass of water into my hands. I slugged down that water, the liquid spilling out of both sides of my mouth and trickling down the front of me. It was delicious!

There was little talking as all the women sat on the benches beneath the trees surrounding the sweat and fire-pit area. I felt free, like I was still flying. Looking down at my glistening, sweaty arms, I saw there were large red splotches all over them. My head was throbbing, and I knew my blood pressure was high. None of it mattered, because the cooling breeze would lower my body temperature and eventually my blood pressure would go down, too.

That second sweat changed my life in many positive ways. I sweated with Patty and her women every day or every other day for six weeks. By the time I left I felt not only like a veteran, but like someone who could stand the hottest of sweats. You see, the Lakota men sweat first with 28 to 30 stones. Then the women follow; to the heated stones still in the pit we add our own 28 to 30 stones. I remember one time when Patty wanted to cleanse herself of some unwanted feelings, she ordered 60 hot, glowing stones, all fresh ones, not leftovers from the earlier men's sweat. Luckily, by then I had had a month's worth of sweats under my belt and I felt confident about going in with her. I was able to last all four rounds without a problem, along with my three Lakota sisters.

Patty taught me about the beauty, the sanctity, the joy and the profound spirituality at sweats. And because the Lakota don't believe in mixed sweats, I was able to discover a wonderful essence of women, of sisters, which I'd never before had the opportunity to explore, much less realize.

Patty was often called by neighbors on the Rosebud or Pine Ridge reservations who had to have surgery or for someone who was dying. She would be asked to hold a sweat and pray for that individual.

MIRACLES OCCUR

Time after time, I saw miracles occur because as few as four or as many as sixteen women would pray for that person—and the prayers would be answered. I saw people who were supposed to die, live. I saw people sail through operations they weren't supposed to survive, or certainly weren't supposed to recover from so quickly. Those six weeks taught me about the intent of prayer in a sweat. I was blessed to be taught by a woman whose heart is pure, who has no ego, and whose walk is her talk.

People were brought by car, by litter and by wheelchair to Patty's sweat. I saw one woman who had to be carried in on a litter because she couldn't walk, so riddled was she with cancer. And I saw this same woman crawl out of that sweat without assistance and stand on her feet for the first time in the year since that disease had begun its ravages. She walked up the very steep hill to Patty's house without help.

I attribute these miracles to the Great Spirit and to a fine team of women who came solely from the heart and who said their prayers with absolute compassion and integrity. As I said, I was a very lucky woman to have been taught by one of the finest women sweat leaders. But then Patty Thomas, Sacred Eagle-Bone Whistle Woman, would just giggle if I told her such a thing, bow her head shyly and say that the Great Spirit was responsible for the healings of the people we prayed for in the sweats. Such is her humility. What a wonderful role model she was for me—and for all women.

HUMILITY IJ THE BEJT TRAIT

I wanted to share this experience because I've heard so many horror stories from women about sweats they've attended where they've had negative experiences. The biggest complaint is usually that the sweat-lodge leader, a male, is egotistical and arrogant. Let me tell you something: Walking the Red Road means walking your talk. The greatest role models we have are those who are the humblest, who show a genuine humility and who take no personal credit for what happens in a sweat.

Another complaint from women is that the sweat-lodge leader flirts with them or tries to grope and touch them in the darkness. That is unconscionable and wrong. Any woman who is ever victimized in a sweat should instantly get up and leave.

Many women have been turned away from participating in a sweat because they were on their moontime (menses). Each tribal nation has taboos or rules about a woman on moontime. I won't get into a debate about this, because as a woman who has a monthly moon, I find it humiliating, angering and downright stupid to be told I can't do something due to this natural and beautiful function. I will say this, any man who has problems with his own inner female will inevitably project that onto women. *They* are the ones who object to women on their moon participating in a sweat.

I've been told I couldn't go to a doctoring ceremony, to a sweat and to other kinds of ceremony because I was on my moon. These battles with brainwashed patriarchal males pushed me into performing sweat ceremonies only for women. I don't care if one of my associates is on her moon when she enters the sweat. What is important is that my sister is there with her heart, her humility and her desire to pray. Over the years I've found that sweats conducted when one or more women are on their moon are inevitably the most powerful. Why? Because we are giving our own blood back to our Mother, the Earth. A giveaway, if you will. We are highly creative and charged with a spiritual energy at this time. We are closer to the veil of the other worlds at this time, and our dreams are more revealing and vivid as a result.

I've been told by a number of medicine men that a woman on her moon steals a man's power. My husband and two other male associates of mine have sweated with me when I was on my moon and they came out more energized, feeling stronger and more whole than at all-male sweats. Further, one of my male companions who conducts mixed sweats always welcomes women on their moon and he's never had a "bad" sweat as a result, and no man ever got sick from it, either.

Complaints of feeling weakened, drained or nauseated after being in a sweat are, unfortunately, common. Either the sweat-lodge leader or someone in the lodge is "stealing" your energy. A good sweat-lodge leader knows how to place adequate protection around those under her/his care during the ceremony. Anyone who doesn't know how to do this or is unable to has no business conducting a sweat lodge. It is that simple. You do not leave your people open and vulnerable to a person who knowingly or unknowingly steals energy during a sweat. If you don't feel good after coming out of a sweat, don't ever go back. Find someone else to conduct them. And pay attention to your feeling about who is going to that sweat with you. If you don't like the feel of one person, or if someone is behaving badly, or if you get a red flag, then turn around and leave. There is no shame in refusing to sweat. As my one teacher told me, don't ever go into a sweat if you don't feel good about it.

THE GLAMOUR OF PHENOMENA

The purpose of a sweat lodge is sacred. Yes, phenomena can occur, but don't get caught up in the glamour of it all. That is not the reason you are there. Spirits of the locality or spirit guides of the sweat leader or others might show up. Sometimes someone will feel the brush of an eagle's wing-tip through her hair or across her cheek as the great bird wings her way around and around within the sweat lodge. Lights resembling the Fourth of July might fly like sparks off the drum of the sweat leader. Things furry or scaled might scamper or slither across your ankles or crossed legs. A spiderweb might be created across the fire pit, and you might see a spider dancing among the red-hot stones. Many sounds can occur—the shriek of the majestic eagle, the hoot of the truth-telling owl or chanting from the spirits who stand in the sweat with you.

You might smell aromas such as sacred cedar, juniper, sage or red willow. The face of a highly regarded spirit might appear in the stones. Or the stone people might begin to sing, and that is one of the most beautiful and moving of all sounds. The top and/or bottom of the lodge might dissolve away and you will see not only the stars above you but also the earth upon which you are sitting. The howl of the wolf might fill the lodge or the sweet, bell-like voice of White Buffalo Calf Woman might waft through the darkness. Sometimes, she or others might appear.

While phenomena like this are exciting to beginners, they mean nothing. The reason for being in a sweat is not to be entertained or awed. The reason you sit in a sweat is to purify yourself spiritually and to pray, both for yourself and for others. Then healing takes place for you as well as for those you are praying for. *That* is why you are in a sweat and for no other reasons.

Too many times I've heard tales of male sweat leaders who try to fry the people in their sweat by trying to make the sweat so hot it chases them out. Sorry, this kind of immature, competitive behavior doesn't fly either. That kind of game-playing is egotistical; it is arrogant and insensitive to the needs of those under the leader's care. The sweat leader has many responsibilities: the protection of all people while in that sweat, the singing of the songs, the correct ceremonial order of each round and the smoking of the pipe. But it is not the sweat-lodge leader's duty to make the sweat a test of physical endurance for personal, egotistical reasons. If there are to be any tests, they will be given by the Great Spirit, and they will always be ones that test your inner courage and strength on some level.

I once attended a sweat where only sixteen stones were used for all four rounds and it was one of the hottest I'd ever experienced. My sixty-stone sweat with Patty felt cool by comparison. The Great Spirit decides what the temperature of that sweat should be for all the participants, not some swollen-headed, arrogant sweat leader. And lest some poorly prepared or ill-trained sweat leader forget, remember that heat raises one's blood pressure and can not only cause a stroke, but can also bring a lawsuit to your door. If you want to prove your manhood, don't do it by making a sweat ungodly hot for your participants.

Anytime I conduct a sweat, I always ask the participants if they have a history of claustrophobia, strokes, heart problems or high blood pressure. In a sweat any and all of these ailments can be triggered. I put those who have claustrophobia near the flap opening so that they know they can leave if they must. If there are new members who have never participated in a sweat before and who have any of these problems, I use fewer stones to keep the temperature at a physically acceptable level. If I feel it's getting too hot, I'll sing fewer songs, open the flap sooner and keep it open longer for them. Again, the idea of a sweat is not to chase people out because they can't take it or to injure them but to give them the sacred space to pray and to heal within.

HELPFUL HINTS

I learned many tricks at Patty's home. I always took in two large towels—one to put over my head and face, if necessary, and one to put across my bare, exposed legs. I wore a simple cotton gown in the sweat, never polyester or any other kind of material. I used to wad up a huge ball of fresh sage and press it against my nose and mouth to breathe through during particularly hot sweats. Just breathing in that wonderful sacred herb was cleansing and healing in itself. I always wore something with long sleeves to protect my lower arms and hands. Never wear a watch or any jewelry into a sweat. The metal heats up and will burn your skin badly.

The steam always shoots to the ceiling of a sweat lodge, then rolls down the sides of the structure. Wise people don't ever sit with their back up against the sweat-lodge wall or poles. Place yourself halfway between the fire pit and the walls; that way the steam won't tunnel down directly on you, but will circulate more freely. If all else fails, you can lie down and get a whiff of the cooler air on the ground. Believe me, there is absolutely no shame in lying on the ground.

In the monthly full-moon sweat I conduct at our home for my associates, we divest ourselves of our garments once we are in the sweat lodge. The towels are still used to protect the sensitive skin of the back of our necks and shoulders. When you know the people in your sweat and they are of the same gender, I see nothing wrong with being naked. However, you should never be naked in a mixed-gender sweat!

If someone in a mixed sweat suggests you disrobe, get up and get out of there. I know that men who sweat together on the reservation disrobe once they are in their sweat lodge, but after the fourth round, they draw a towel around their hips as they emerge from the lodge.

Being unclothed during a sweat is as close, symbolically, as any of us can get to feeling what it was like to be a tiny baby inside our mother's womb. A sweat is dark and moist, a reminder of our mother's womb, where we spent nine months developing in a safe and warm place. As adults, we can sit naked, the sweat running off our bodies, the fertile Earth beneath us, and create that womblike sensation once again. Only this time, if all things are right in the sweat, we will experience the heartbeat of Mother Earth. We are reminded that we are children of her heart and that we are greatly loved by her.

A sweat lodge is a sacred place devoid of egos, power trips, power plays and power over others. It is about spiritual cleansing, being loved by our Mother and praying. One should never leave a sweat feeling out of sorts, drained, weak, hurting, humiliated, victimized or ashamed. If for whatever reason you can't last all four rounds, there is no shame in this. Look at how long you were able to stay and see the positive side of it. In a true sweat, neither the leader nor the participants will see you as weak or dishonorable. It is not failure, but a learning experience. There is shame only in making a person feel bad for leaving.

In one sweat, my newest associate had to leave after the third round had just begun. She hadn't told me she was claustrophobic. After she murmured, "Mitakuye oyasin," I stopped singing and drumming and asked my sisters to help her move clockwise around the sweat in order to leave. Many pairs of hands fell upon my sister as she slowly worked her way around the fire pit. Later, after we all emerged, each woman went over to her, hugged her and congratulated her for staying so long for a first time. I told her that next time I would place her next to the flap where she would receive more air, and she walked away from her experience feeling good about herself. She felt that she'd taken a huge step in conquering her claustrophobia by being able to stay until the third round. I feel she did, too.

There should never be any kind of monetary charge to conduct a sweat, because it is a gift from the Great Spirit to all of us. If you want to gift the sweat-lodge leader, then do so with whatever you feel is appropriate. I always tell people that if they must give me something, they can make a donation to their favorite charity in my name.

On the reservation food is usually given as a gift or sometimes a blanket or some other utilitarian present. I saw Patty Thomas give many sacks of groceries, clothes and other essentials for life to those less fortunate than herself. She constantly gave to the poor of her people, and I honor her for that generosity. But then a true sweat-lodge leader embodies all that is good and right about the Red Road: humility, generosity and selflessness.

The Ant People

I was taught to respect all things as my relatives — even insects. One would never stomp on a relative just for getting under foot or being pesky. Instead, if an ant crawled on my foot, I was to pay attention to her visit, not reach out and smack her.

Visitation by the Great Spirit's relatives is important, although to the average "asleep" individual, it might appear as an irritation. Anytime one of our relatives comes to us three times, then we must pay special attention and understand that it is bringing a message to us. What kind? In order to know, we must place ourselves into communication with that relative and find out.

Most people will scoff at the idea that we can communicate with our brethren, be they animal, insect, plant or rock — but we can. Unfortunately, most people in America are taught to be strictly left-brained; everything must be seen, weighed, measured or somehow physically proved in order to exist in our reality.

RIGHT-BRAINED UNDERSTANDING

Native American people are just naturally, genetically, right-brained. The right hemisphere of the brain is tied into the cosmos and all the dimensions that interweave our space. The left hemisphere's whole mission is to keep us grounded in the third dimension, our physical reality. However, the right brain is there so we can switch to it in order to become part of the much larger macrocosm that flows around us without end.

The River of Life, that seemingly invisible (to our left brain and physical eyes) rainbow-colored energy that ebbs and flows through and around us, is our medium for transporting thoughts, feelings, instinct and intuition between ourselves and our relatives. This is the conveyance by which we can communicate with anything else, seen or unseen, that thrives here on Mother Earth. Everything is based upon sound vibration, and the River of Life is no different, having a frequency of its own.

We can close our eyes, which diminishes the left-brain function, take three deep breaths into the nose and out of the eyes and make the switch to the right brain. Once that is accomplished, we can mentally send a thought, a picture or a feeling from the heart to whomever we wish to contact, whether it's another human or one of our relatives; the telepathic feeling will then arrive.

Our relatives are sensitized to this vibrational communication. I can't say the same for us humans who have allowed our left brains to encroach too deeply to the territory that belongs to our right brains. As a result, we're about as thick as concrete and just as responsive, unable to hear the communications from our relatives. A few of us are aware of such contact. With some practice, we can all become more in touch with the world around us.

My teacher always called the insects "Little People" and I've always liked the term. They *are* little in comparison to our gigantic size. We probably look like dinosaurs to them! When I was learning to make my first rattle, my teacher took me out to a red anthill and crouched down. He gave them an offering of cornmeal, which they readily received with great thanks. And then he proceeded to tell me about the Ant People.

First of all, 99.9% of ants are female. They're just like the Bee People, who keep only a few male drones to impregnate the queen. (So these are my sisters — females, too.) The Ant People are such wonderful teachers if we would just take fifteen minutes out of our busy schedules and simply watch them. They could teach us much about community and serving one another unselfishly. Alone, they can lift many times their body weight; but together as a cohesive, coordinated unit, they can carry a dead bird to their mound.

Ant People are garbage cans of a sort — they will eat almost anything, or store it for their winter use. However, at our place we have about five red anthills and we've found some interesting variations. Some of the colonies will eagerly eat and store the fresh fruit from our trees when they are gifted with it. Other colonies won't touch the fruit, yet they will welcome meat of any kind, be it other insects, a dead snake, bird or mouse. After I noticed this, it made sense to me that each mound would prefer a different food, for that way no one source would be depleted (perhaps forcing some of the ants to starve for lack of that specific food).

LIVING IN HARMONY

When we first moved to the Sedona area, one of our well-meaning white neighbors came over with a huge, deadly can of ant powder. My husband, who happened to be working near one mound at the time, saw the man stoop over to deliver the killing powder to the first mound. With a shout, he asked him to stop. Bewildered, our neighbor straightened.

"Hey, you got to kill these pests."

"My wife's Cherokee, and we believe in living in harmony with everything," my husband said.

The neighbor smiled a little. "They'll overrun this place. I promise you that."

"I don't think they will."

"Oh?"

"Yes, she talks to them."

The neighbor lost his smile. "Well," he muttered a little defiantly, "you're going to be sorry. These damned ants will be in your house, in your food, and you'll never get rid of them."

My husband stood there and didn't respond but merely thanked the neighbor for his concern. None of our anthills were harmed. When my husband related the incident to me, I felt sad. If only this neighbor would realize what a service the Ant People provide for an area. They are scavengers who clean the ground of relatives who have died. In a sense, they are like the buzzard and vulture — people who are the garbage trucks of the air and clean the land of large, dead animals.

We have so much waste in this world of ours, and yet we continue to kill off the very relatives who help us clean it up. I have seen Ant People take a dead tarantula apart, one leg at a time, and finally drag its heavy, massive body over to their hole. Within hours the tarantula was dismantled and taken down into their food chambers. Many kinds of seeds, often seen as weeds, are also carried into the hills. Without the Ant People doing this, we'd be overrun with weeds. Fruit that is not picked drops to the ground and rots. The Ant People come along and clean off Mother Earth's surface by taking the rotting fruit underground for use.

ANT CRYSTALS

As the Ant People carve out their food chambers, they bring small stones to the surface. One can find them all around a hill. We Native Americans revere these stones and consider them very powerful. First of all, they have been touched and blessed by the Ant People. Secondly, they come from within our Mother. Most of these stones contain quartz crystal, and we acknowledge that the Crystal People are powerful teachers for us.

As my teacher crouched with me near the anthill, he told me to gift them with food and ask if I might take a few ant crystals for the rattle I was making.

I gave the ants some scraps of meat and fruit and mentally sent my request to them. Almost instantly I received a warm, emphatic "yes!" I did not take many pebbles, for I was taught never to be greedy about such things. My teacher directed me to choose four rose quartz or pink stones. He said that these four would give me the protection I would sometimes need while working ceremonially.

When we moved to our home, the first thing I did was take gifts of food and cornmeal to each of our five red anthills. I crouched by each one, taking care not to step on any of my sisters, and laid the food around the hole. I told them my name and that we were honored to have them with us as we became custodians of this land. I asked that they respect our home and not enter it. If they would respect my request, I would make sure that they would remain safe and well-fed.

I went to each anthill with the same greeting, gift and request. To this day, four years later, not one red ant has ever entered our home – or bitten us. When I'm outside I always pay attention to where I place my feet because I don't want to kill one of my ant sisters accidentally. Sometimes it happens, and then I pray for the Great Spirit to take her over the Rainbow Bridge so that she may continue her evolution unimpeded. Many times while I'm working in the orchard or rose garden, my ant sisters will climb onto my shoes, walk up my pant leg and come to visit me. Never once have they bitten me, for they know I will not harm them.

MESSENGERS FROM THE SUBCONSCIOUS

Because the Ant People live beneath the surface of Mother Earth, which is considered the unconscious or subconscious from the point of view of Jungian psychology, they have a special communion with our real Mother and can bring messages from Mother Earth directly to us, to our conscious minds. So we say that the Ant People's power is great. There are few relatives who live both beneath and on the surface of our Mother.

A person with Ant Medicine has the ability to bring information from her own subconscious, her subterranean structure, to the light of her consciousness. This is quite a feat in itself, believe me, because most of us are pretty much numb to the subtle voices of our subconscious. If we want to blossom and grow spiritually, that link with our subconscious must be made and maintained. Receiving Ant Medicine will help this become so.

As I sit here writing this article, one of my black ant sisters has just crawled up my right leg and onto the computer desk and is now moving back and forth across the keyboard. I love the double checks, the blessings that are there when we walk in perfect harmony with the Great Spirit's intentions. The black ant sister was sent to approve of what is being written and shared with our relatives. It's not uncommon for them to show up when something is happening, and this is a very good sign that what you are doing is right for you.

For six months out of the year the Ant People live within Mother Earth and never come to the surface. This is their hibernation time, much like that of the Bear People, who have their own ways of withdrawing into Mother Earth to sleep and dream — only Ant People don't sleep! They are energetically doing their thing in total darkness within our Mother. Able to sense subtle changes in weather and temperature, they come out of the subconsciousness of Mother Earth when the time is right.

Ant Medicine bestows upon a person a sense of greater mission and awareness of her/his fellow two-leggeds and other relatives. For instance, each summer our fruit trees are heavy with bounty, and like the Ant People, we can store much of the crop. At the same time, we fill boxes with fruit and take it to the mission in Cottonwood for those who are less fortunate than ourselves. That fruit feeds the elderly, those with fixed incomes and those who are forced to be on welfare. Nothing is ever hoarded but shared with the community as a whole.

People who are involved in their neighborhood, their town, their state or country usually have Ant Medicine. They realize they are not separate from the rest and use their voices, ideas and votes to become part of that inseparable matrix that binds all of us to one another. People who volunteer several hours a week or month to worthy projects also have Ant Medicine. A food co-op, for example, is much like a communal anthill, where all people who are members receive the bounty of everyone's hard work.

Those who are strongly family oriented and take care of their elders, instead of sending them to a nursing home, have Ant Medicine, too. There is nothing stronger than an ant community, for they pull together – in the same direction – as a unit. They perform miracles every day as a group in situations where a single individual could never succeed.

I once saw a dead mouse near an anthill. As a group, the ants had worked to separate the head of the mouse from the the heavier body. There must have been fifty ants, all working in unison to carry that head over to the hill's opening. I marveled at their strength, their spirit, their sense of continuity and their connectedness with one another. They all somehow knew to move in the same direction at the same time. It was an engineering feat and a miracle. I have asked myself if I move with such coordination in my own walk in life and have had a great deal to reflect upon as a result.

The Ant People are wonderful teachers we can watch and then draw parallels within our own lives. Are we connected to other people? To our families? Do we honor our neighbors and help them out when they need us? Is there something each of us can do within the scope of our neighborhoods for the larger good of the community as a whole? Or do we shun others, preferring to live in a vacuum that is very self-serving? The Ant People teach us generosity of spirit, sharing, giving and receiving. They help us comprehend the saying, "As above, so below." I can think of no finer aspiration than to be antlike.

Spirit Guides

$\mathcal{I}$ had an interesting conversation with O'Ryin Swanson, publisher of the *Sedona Journal of Emergence!* We sat over lunch discussing some new and very exciting information that Vywamus has passed along via Barbara Burns in regard to devas and their intrinsic importance to our spiritual evolutionary journey while in physical form. The more O'Ryin shared with me about these revelations [see "Becoming a Descended Master" in the March 1993 issue], the more I smiled.

I was taught by Sam, my Cherokee teacher, that each person, whether Indian or not, has a chief guide, or spirit guide. I had always likened my spirit guide to the Christian idea of a guardian angel, who is always there to help us, counsel us and in general keep us out of hot water – provided we listen to the voice of our spirit guide, or our intuition, our knowing, if you will. The spirit guide to us is a deva to those who follow other metaphysical disciplines.

True, the angelic kingdom is a separate kingdom from what I'm going to share with you, but this is the closest I can come from my own shamanic/Cherokee training to giving those outside of my view of the world an idea of what I am talking about.

ONE CHIEF SPIRIT GUIDE

Let's start at the beginning. I was taught that each person has a spirit guide, a chief one, who oversees one's development during this lifetime. This spirit guide, at least for those of Native American heritage (and I will stick my neck out and suggest that it is also true for those people who have had strong incarnations as North or South American Indian), always comes in the guise of an animal, insect, reptile or plant.

I remember one conversation with Sam about chief spirit guides. One of my friends had told me that his was a Bald Eagle. I was taught to look at what the animal, in this case a bird, symbolized. My teacher told me to look at the guide in the context of what it was, what it did and how it moved within the flow of the River of Life that surrounds all of us, whether we're two-leggeds, four-leggeds, winged ones, crawlies, plants or Little People (the insect kingdom). When my teacher told me this, I know I gave him a very perplexed look. He asked me what the bald eagle did and I replied, "It flies."

"What else?" he prompted.

I searched frantically for a better answer, for flying was obvious.

"Well . . . uh, it flies higher than any other bird in the world."

"That's true. What else?"

I began to sweat. What else did an eagle do? "Uh," I stammered, "it eats fish because it's a sea eagle."

"Yes. What else?"

Frantic, I seesawed between anger toward my teacher for being so pedantic and desperation because I was trying to please him by coming up with the right answer. I didn't like this kind of prodding, but he just patiently stood there, looking at me while I sweated.

"Let's see . . ." I rolled my eyes upward to Father Sky, searching for the answer. I wrestled for nearly five minutes, the silence growing heavy between us. He finally took pity on me.

"How does it hunt?"

Wiping the sweat off my face, I scrunched up my brow. "The eagle flies high to see the fish in the water and then swoops down to grab it out of the water with its claws."

"Good," he praised.

"Thank goodness," I thought.

"But what else?"

I grimaced and gave him a pleading look. "I don't know what else."

He smiled. "Sometimes surrendering is better than scrambling for an answer."

Grinning sheepishly, I acknowledged his wisdom. If I'd been honest with myself, I'd have said from the beginning that I didn't know. That's at least surrendering over to the truth, which is something he was trying to teach me to do. I remembered another old adage: "Pride goeth before a fall." Well, I had a fall.

Sam gestured to the sky. "What is the bald eagle's strongest point? What does he do best besides fly?"

I thought and thought. Finally, in a moment of desperate inspiration I said, "His eyes! He's got excellent vision."

Sam's smile broadened significantly. "Yes!"

Catching his enthusiasm, I began waving my hands around because that's what I do when I'm excited or trying to explain something either to myself or another person. "An eagle's eyes are the most important. So are you saying a person whose chief spirit guide is an eagle has good eyes?"

"Now, the whole reason you get a spirit guide is to become like them," Sam counseled.

"Oh, that means the person might not see things well, then?"

"Yes, but the eagle will teach the person how to see things better and with more depth or perception and, perhaps, clarity."

Excited, I nodded, beginning to grasp the relationship he wanted me to understand.

"So the bald eagle would be a symbol, telling this person to aspire to become like the bird?"

"Yes." He gave me a look of praise. "Remember, when we become aware of our chief spirit guide, the real training, the changes and transformation begin to take place."

"But," I struggled, "what if the person doesn't want to see? Or what if she doesn't want to learn to "fly" above a situation to see it more clearly?"

Sam thought for a moment. "The chief spirit guide is with us from the moment we're born until we leave our physical form and even after that in some cases. This bald eagle wouldn't force his or her human counterpart to change if that individual didn't want to. A chief spirit guide is there to be listened to through our inner voice, heart, feelings and intuition. If we choose not to listen, then that's our problem."

"And then," I guessed, "those people will run into a lot of road blocks and walls in their lives?"

"Yes."

"Sam, what else could this bald eagle possibly represent?"

He grinned and squinted at me from where he crouched on the ground. Scooping up some dirt, he allowed it to sift through his large, weathered hands. "What do you feel about it?"

I groaned and plopped down in front of him, my legs crossed. "I knew you were going to answer a question with a question!"

Laughing, he continued to sift the dirt, handling it as if it were a very much loved child. "So? What do you feel?"

THE MEANING OF FLYING

Grumpily, I stared down at Mother Earth, my chin resting in the palms of my hands. "It flies. So, what does flying mean symbolically?" I was thinking out loud so he could see my thought process. "Flying could mean rising above a situation to see it more clearly. Or it could mean letting go of my own reality, teachings given to me by school, parents or religion. If I could do that, maybe I could perceive my situation, whatever it was, in a new or different light. A better one?" I twisted a look up at his darkly tanned face. I saw the wrinkles at the corners of his eyes grow pronounced, so I knew he was pleased with my answer – thus far. Sighing, I went on. "There's the saying that if you stick with the turkeys, you'll never fly like an eagle."

Sam laughed out loud, the deep, resonating sound echoing around the canyon where we sat. "So what does that mean?"

"That if I have this chief spirit guide, I'm supposed to reevaluate my parental conditioning process and the environment I've been raised in and look at my philosophy to see what can be thrown out and what can be kept."

"Why?"

"I knew you were going to ask that," I said unhappily, giving him a dirty look. He was smiling, so I knew I was on the right track. After ruminating for several minutes, I said, "The whole Native American experience is about learning to be always in harmony and in balance within ourselves," I said. "And to do this we must remember that not everything we were taught or were trapped within helps us to achieve that goal. In order to do it, we must let go of these things that hinder us, keep us unbalanced or stop us from growing."

"Right so far. Go on," he drawled.

Quirking my lips, I muttered, "That's so easy for you to say."

"Wait until you have students of your own," he said, smiling.

I wasn't thinking of my students. In fact, I'd never thought along those lines. I gave him a startled look, but I saw his eyes grow distant and I knew he wasn't going to say any more than he already had. "Okay," I groused belligerently, "the key word here is "transformation," with the goal being our own unique balance and harmony within ourselves. So, if I got a bald eagle for a chief spirit guide, I'd probably have to look very closely at my upbringing and beliefs and begin to honestly throw out what was no longer useful to me or stopped me from growing spiritually. The eagle would help me rise above my own limitations, to see more clearly in order to make better choices that would help me grow in a positive way."

"Very good. What about the bald eagle flying higher than any other bird?"

"You've always said that eagles flew higher than anyone else and that they had the ear of the Great Spirit because of that. They're also messengers."

"That's right. How would you interpret that?"

BEING IN TOUCH WITH THE GREAT SPIRIT

Groaning, I said, "If I transformed, grew and listened to my own inner guidance, to my heart through which the chief spirit guide speaks, I might communicate more closely with the Great Spirit?"

"Yes." Sam slowly unwound his lean, tall form and stood up. He had a piece of grass stuck in the corner of his mouth. He was chewing on it thoughtfully. "Not only that, but if you work hard, listen and walk through your fear of transformation, you may someday become a messenger from the Great Spirit to others." He looked down at me and his eyes twinkled. "That is a very honored and humbling position to be in."

"Very," I murmured. I stood up and brushed the seat of my pants off, knowing the day's lesson was finished. Sam was a very powerful Cherokee medicine man, but he was humble about it too, and I was always conscious that those who had real power were the humblest of us all. At least those who were walking in harmony had left their egos behind and moved with the flow of the River of Life.

DISCOVERING MY SPIRIT GUIDE

I didn't have to worry about having an eagle for a chief spirit guide. I had discovered mine nearly twenty years ago when I came upon a blue-gray wingtip feather. You see, we all have a chief spirit guide, a deva, if you will, who is our mentor throughout our lifetime. Sometimes we'll see this chief spirit guide in physical form. For instance, you might see a squirrel three times in a very short amount of time, perhaps days, or see a red-tail hawk three days in a row, or a coyote.

That is how the devic kingdom talks to us — either though physical manifestation, showing up in our lives three times in a row, or by coming to us in a dream, vision or meditation. Native Americans always put great stock in the number three, and if we see anything three times in a row, we pay attention. We realize this animal is trying first, to get our attention; second, to "talk" to us; and third, to get us to take the symbolic form and apply it to our lives. Let me give you an example.

I was walking one night with my husband, arm in arm, on the fifteen-acre Arabian horse farm we had in Lisbon, Ohio. Naturally, our nine horses were following us, single file, as we took our evening stroll. It was a time to talk with my husband, trade what had happened during the day and, in general, have "quality time" with one another. On this particular evening it was near dusk as we walked the large oval fields. I spotted a long gray-blue feather. Enchanted, I rushed forward to look at it. How beautiful and huge it was! My husband came and looked at it as well. My heart began pounding — I didn't know why at the time.

I trembled all over, and a good kind of excitement came over me as I leaned over to look at it more closely. I was struck by its lovely pale blue color. I had no idea what kind of feather it was, but I did know that it was significant. As I reached down, I told my husband that if I picked up the feather, my life would begin to change drastically. I didn't know why I'd said that or why I knew that; I simply knew it to be true. And without hesitation, I gently picked up the "finger feather." The moment I did, a great blue heron flashed in front of the view screen located in the center of my head. I told my husband that this feather belonged to a great blue heron.

THE GREAT BLUE HERON

He reminded me that the small creek that flowed through our property always had a great blue heron who fished in it. I stood there, my fingertips tingling as I lightly stroked that incredibly long, lovely feather. It was then that I remembered: I would often be out on the swing under the cottonwood tree in the evenings, just absorbing the ending of the day, when a great blue heron would fly in with her magnificent seven-foot wingspan and land in the creek just below our farmhouse. She had been doing that for seven years in a row, but I hadn't realized why she kept visiting me. I guess I was too dense and didn't get the message from her showing up, so she had to drop a wingtip feather in the pasture to get my attention.

It has been many years since I picked up that feather. And I was right; my life did change dramatically. Within a year, my teacher, Sam, came into my life. The great blue heron, I found out later, was my chief spirit guide, and since then I've been learning how to become a great blue heron in my life. The devic kingdom embraces all of the Great Spirit's animals, insects, reptiles, plants, rocks, water, and even Mother Earth herself. Why should we not be able to learn and grow through that which nurtures us the most? Mother Earth is our *true* mother. She feeds us, clothes us and cares for us. When Native Americans say, "All our relatives" or "All my relations," we mean simply that we are all interconnected with one another – without exception.

THE RIVER OF LIFE UNITES US

In the previous chapter I talked about the concept of the River of Life, that this invisible (to our naked eyes) rainbow-colored energy flows in, around and through us, permeating every cell of our bodies. It touches all forms of life and this includes Mother Earth herself. That is how we are bound to one another, and what we do to ourselves sends out a vibrational frequency that affects many others on many other levels, both seen and unseen.

We all have a great chief spirit guide. If you'd like to know how to get in touch with yours, think back and ask yourself, "What has happened to me three times in a row in a very short time?" If you can't think of anything, then tell your subconscious just before you go to sleep at night, "I want my chief spirit guide to contact me through a dream." Do this for at least 30 days. It might not happen at first, but eventually your perseverance will be rewarded. Or if you meditate, ask the same thing and see what happens. Another, perhaps easier, way is to have a shaman journey for you and find out on your behalf, keeping in mind that he/she must have permission to do it — from you and from a higher authority! If you are indeed sincere about knowing who your chief spirit guide is, your question will be answered eventually. Part of the Red Road experience is learning patience and endurance.

LEJJER JPIRIT GUIDEJ

There is a hierarchy I was taught that coincides with what Vywamus has shared through Barbara Burns. Besides the deva or chief spirit guide, there is a lesser pantheon of spirit guides for us, also in animal form, that come and go in our lives. These transitory devas/animal spirit guides are less powerful than the chief deva/spirit guide, but they come into our lives to teach us an individual skill that we're ready to learn. Now, we might not consciously be aware that we're ready to learn this new thing. I try to pay attention to what it is. I then ask myself, "What does this guide symbolize? How can I apply it to my own experience right now?"

Let me give you an example. Let's say a flicker comes into my life, and that I see this bird three times in a row on the same day. First, I would go to the library and read up on this bird to find out what her characteristics are. Once I found out, I'd ask myself how they apply to me. For instance, a flicker survives by having a long, narrow beak that bores holes into the bark of trees to find little bugs hiding in there. From a symbolic standpoint, it would mean focus, wouldn't it? Drilling in one spot to create a hole to go after a particular thing or goal is certainly focus, intensity and single-minded purpose, isn't it? The promise of the flicker is this: If I concentrate on one thing long enough, with patience and endurance, I will get the "gift" of the food/bug. I would look at what I'm currently doing in my life and ask, "What do I need to concentrate on single-mindedly until I complete the task and get the gift?" Such is the lesson of the flicker if she enters your life. There are many other symbolisms regarding the flicker, but this one will suffice as an example. When you have learned the new skill or lesson, the lesser spirit guide leaves you. Then, at some point in the future, the deva will bring another one into your life to symbolize the next rung on the ladder of your growth.

A good resource for understanding some of the symbolism is Medicine Cards, as well as your own footwork at the local library and asking naturalists, zoo keepers or people who know the specific animal's traits.

CHANGE IS OUR RESPONSIBILITY

The chief spirit guide is there to help us, guide us and speak to us in the language of the right brain — the heart, feelings and intuition, or inner voice. If we elect to transform and grow, then other spirit guides will be asked to come to us to teach us certain new skills, embellish a talent, nurture us or support us in some new endeavor. However if we allow fear to stop us, the chief spirit guides cannot force us to change — that's not their responsibility. It's ours. A chief spirit guide's responsibility is to be there to support us and act as an inner counsel for us. They also bring in other teachers, new spirit guides, as we grow to a place where we can expand, add to our skills or develop new ones.

All of these phenomena are deva-based — the spirit guides, the River of Life, our Mother Earth. Having the courage to break the hold of the fear(s) that stops us from being all that we can be is up to us. I can tell you unequivocally that there is a cheering section for each of you, unseen, who are rooting nonstop for you to "leap tall buildings in a single bound." If you have the courage to make the change, the inner support will be there.

THE ROSE DEVAS

Besides a personal group of spirit guides for each of us, there are also devas all over Mother Earth who function in harmony with her and all our relations. Let me give you an example. I have a large rose garden, most of the plants being tree roses or huge rose bushes. There is a deva who is in charge of the entire group of rose bushes, some forty of them. Each rose bush has its own spirit. These individual spirits work willingly with the deva who oversees them. The deva is nurturing, supportive and helpful. The *elementals*, less evolved forms of spiritual energy who most often appear to be balls of light, flow in the River of Life. The Rose Garden Deva makes sure that elemental energy is there to "feed" each individual rose bush and also to ensure the continual flow of the River of Life energy through and around each rose bush. My job is to water the roses, prune them and give them fish fertilizer.

I'm in mental contact with the Rose Garden Deva. As I go around to each rose bush, I touch the plant, talk to it, praise it and tell it how beautiful it is. I can feel each rose plant respond with such incredible love that it brings tears to my eyes. Every day I go out there and touch them, love them and praise them. So, I'm doing more than just watering and giving them fertilizer. The rose bushes flower from February through November each year! Granted, I live in Arizona, but we're at 3500 feet and we get snow sometimes, so believe me, roses blooming in November is a minor miracle in itself!

ROCK PEOPLE

Every time you see a mountain, remember there is a mountain deva who is charged with caring for all the Rock People, each of whom has a spirit – so you know there are millions of devas, one for each of the rocks that make up a mountain! Each vicinity on Mother Earth has a deva who is in charge, who ensures the harmony, the flow of the River of Life through that area. A river has a deva, just as a stream has a spirit. The larger the river, the more powerful the deva. The larger the mountain, the more powerful the deva, and so on. We have a fifty-tree fruit orchard, and there is a Fruit Tree Deva who is there to help nurture each of those trees.

You all have devas where you live. Each tree has a living spirit in it, each rock, each flower, each bush. If you'd like to contact a deva, I'll share with you what I was taught.

CONTACTING A DEVA

1. Start in your own back yard. Go outside when you feel at peace with yourself – don't do this if you're angry, upset or distracted. What this demands of you is flicker medicine: single-minded purpose and concentration. Take a braid of sweetgrass and light it. Wave it around the area. Sweetgrass is a "perfume" to devas and elementals – they love the aroma of it. Elementals will eagerly come because they see you are honoring, respecting and gifting them.

2. Burn at least half a rope of sweetgrass and then close your eyes. Take three deep breaths, into the nostrils and out of the mouth. Center yourself. Give your name (a very important thing to do) and tell the spirits that you have come to gift and honor them. Then, wait. The Cherokee have a great saying: "Expect nothing, receive

everything." Just wait. After about twenty minutes, open your eyes, burn the rest of the sweetgrass rope and say, "Thank you for coming. I honor you." Have a notebook with you so you can journal your experience: any sensations, emotions, physical or mental responses, colors, symbols or words spoken. Write them down.

PATIENCE IS THE KEY

3. You might have to do this at least three times before anything happens. I'm not going to tell you what can happen, because I don't want to set you up psychologically. Many devas and elementals have been hurt and injured by man, so at this point they are naturally distrustful of most human beings on first encounter. However if you show them your intent by gifting them with sweetgrass, then that's a signal that you're safe and that you're coming from the heart. Gradually, they will come closer and closer. The elementals are highly curious and will probably be the first to "touch" you. The devas are more circumspect because they are much more evolved, more watchful and really do know what lies in your heart and whether you are sincere about contacting them. A deva will know your true intent. So, if you're doing this out of curiosity or for selfish purposes, they'll never come up and introduce themselves to you. However if you are sincere, a deva will test you – for how long, it's hard to say. They want to make sure you want to contact them. Patience is the key here.

4. Another way to draw elementals and devas to you is to sing them songs or play a musical instrument for them. They love singing! You can light the sweetgrass and hum or sing. I use a drum, and I also have a flute I play (poorly, believe me, but it's the intent that counts).

5. Once you have made contact with the deva, ask what you can do for it. Would it like you to come once a week and sing a song? Play a drum or some other musical instrument for it? Dance with it? Meditate and visualize a certain color in harmony with it? The possibilities are endless. In return a deva can become your teacher, but this isn't something you ask, expect or demand from them. In order to get, you've got to give. You have to prove to the deva that you're coming sincerely from your heart and want nothing except to give the outpouring of love, respect and honor that comes from the deepest part of you.

6. I was also taught to leave gifts of food behind – not meat,

either! Rather, grain, seed and berries, so that the deva can call to the birds, squirrels, chipmunks or mice to share in the gift, too. By giving you will automatically, over time, receive something of equal (and usually greater) value. Be open and receptive.

7. If a deva takes you "under her wing" many wonderful and positive things can happen. It is like teamwork — you help one another. There is a sense of sharing and joy like none other you have experienced. Further, a deva can "talk" to you in your dreams, in meditation, in a vision or, if you're clairvoyant, you'll feel it impressing you with mental telepathy and feelings.

THE SEQUOIA DEVA

I have one last experience about a Sequoia Deva that I'd like to share with you. Many years ago Sam sent me to the sequoia groves up above Bakersfield, California. I had an incredible experience with one particular sequoia spirit. He gave me his name and asked if he could work with me. I said yes. A week after I returned home to Lisbon, Ohio, one of my favorite horses, Molly, got colic, which is a "stomachache," only a lot more dangerous.

Molly rolled and flailed around in the paddock next to the barn, grunting and groaning. I was beside myself with terror, because I knew she didn't have just plain old colic but a deadly form known as "twisted gut colic" that usually ends up killing a horse. The only way a horse could be saved was an expensive (thousands of dollars) operation. But we lived so far out in the country, and I knew our veterinarian didn't have the facilities to perform such an operation. I ran to the house to call Dick, our vet. His assistant said he was out on another emergency call. I'm afraid I wasn't cool, calm or collected. I sobbed into the phone that Dick had to come right now! I slammed down the phone and tore back out to the paddock where Molly was continuing to roll in horrible agony.

I tried to stop Molly from rolling, because in twisted gut colic, it only makes the situation worse. However trying to stop a one thousand-pound horse from rolling when I was only 140 pounds — not to mention the flailing, deadly hooves — is no easy task. I didn't succeed. Frantically, I tugged and pulled on her halter, trying to get her to stand and walk, which would have helped. But Molly was in such pain that all she could do was roll, groan and grunt. Twenty minutes passed. Molly had broken out in a heavy sweat, her skin glistening. I raced back to the house and called the vet again. He was still out. This time I shrieked at the receptionist to get him here or Molly was going to die!

AJK FOR HELP

I ran back to the paddock, knowing that Molly was going to die. I was crying so much by the time I reached her that I stumbled and fell into the dirt beside her. Molly stopped only momentarily, heaving for breath, groaning, her eyes rolling back in her head. The moment I tried to get her up, she started rolling again. Forty-five minutes passed. By this time, Molly was getting tired, foam covering her chest and flanks, but she still rolled ceaselessly. I called the vet a third time. He was on his way! I ran back out to the paddock, terrified, knowing it was too late.

Molly lay on her side panting and groaning, so weak now that she was resting between bouts of rolling. Sobbing so hard I couldn't see, I fell down between her legs and placed both my hands on her belly. I was desperate; I would try anything. I called to the Sequoia Deva and asked for his help. The instant I asked, I saw an incredible green light snaking up and out of Mother Earth right under us and moving up through my body and out of my hands. I watched in amazement as the green light flooded in weblike strands all across Molly's belly. My sobbing stopped. My tears dried. I knelt there feeling incredible energy pumping up through me, vibrating me; I saw it completely encircle Molly's belly. I vaguely heard Molly give an ommphhhh. The mare suddenly groaned, released a long sigh through her nostrils, and then, miraculously, she relaxed. Her entire body went slack. Horrified, my eyes flew open and I looked at her, thinking she'd died. Her eyes were half open, and she was still alive.

The green light began to thin out to a trickle, and in another five minutes, it had disappeared. I heard my Sequoia Deva tell me that Molly would be fine. Sniffling, I lifted my trembling hands from her belly and watched her. She was utterly relaxed, breathing normally and no longer in pain. I could scarcely believe it.

Then I realized that in my state of high anxiety, I'd forgotten to ask for help. I'd been so upset, I'd forgotten to ask anybody. I knelt there by Molly in a state of shock. I didn't know tree devas could do something like this. Gathering my wits, I stumbled to my feet and rushed back to the farmhouse to tell the vet that he didn't have to come.

As I hurried back to the paddock after making the five-minute call, my heart stopped. Molly was gone! She was not in the paddock. How could that be? Panicked, I ran into the barn. There, in the stall, Molly was contentedly munching on hay. My mouth fell open. I just couldn't believe it. Anyone who owns horses or has had a colicky one knows that they never eat right after a colic – it takes hours for them to get over their stomachache. I rushed into the stall, hands shaking as I touched Molly in disbelief. She was no longer sweating. She wasn't nervous or exhausted at all. I stood there, absolutely stunned. I knew then that the Sequoia Deva had healed Molly completely and to the point where she appeared never to have had the colic in the first place!

I heard the screech of tires entering the barn driveway. It was the vet. What was I going to tell him? I heard him slam the door. He was running toward the barn entrance. I ran to meet him. Dick halted, bag in hand, wide-eyed and breathing hard. I threw up my hands and told him it was all right. And then I stammered through an explanation, leaving out the healing portion, of course.

"It's impossible for Molly to recover that quickly," he told me as we hurried to her stall. Taking out his stethoscope, Dick listened intently to her stomach for gut sounds, an indication that the colic was gone. I stood there tensely, watching him closely as he checked her belly, checked her heart rate, looked at her eyes and walked around her with a scowl.

"Well," Dick muttered, "this just can't be."

"What can't?"

"She's fine. It's as though you were making up the story. There's no sign of colic. Her gut sounds are normal. Her heart rate is normal and so is her breathing." He gave me a searching look. Dick and I had been working together for almost five years, and he knew that I was competent in vetting my horses and would never lie to him about something like this. I felt my face getting very red and hot and shrugged my shoulders. "I guess it's a miracle, Dick." And it was a Sequoia Deva miracle.

The Tree People

Over twenty years ago a woman named Sandy came into my life. She was a psychic and way ahead of her time in terms of the idea of getting back in touch with Mother Earth. I had met her casually in Cleveland, Ohio, while visiting my friend and associate, Karen David, who lived in nearby Solon. I went to one of Sandy's workshops and was very impressed with her enthusiasm and energy. To make a long story very short, Sandy contacted me many months later and asked if I'd like to be part of a group of women she was gathering to go to the sequoias at Giant Forest Lodge east of Bakersfield, California.

I asked Sandy why we would be going, and she said that she wanted seven women who had a commitment to meditating and working as a group among the sequoias. It sounded great to me because nature meant automatic healing to my soul, so I said to count me in. I also asked her if my dear friend, Laura Weigt, a registered nurse who was in her sixties, could come along, too. Sandy said yes.

WORKING WITH WOMEN

Before this invitation to work within a group of women, I had always been a loner in many respects. I hadn't yet gotten the message about working with women, either. I was just sort of hanging in a no-person's land doing my own thing, which, at that time, was medical astrology and homeopathy. I hadn't yet picked up the great blue heron feather, which was to change the course of my life and bring Sam, my Cherokee mentor, into it. By choosing to walk the Red Road ever since, I've gotten powerfully in touch with my own feminine side, and I often work with women and women's groups. But looking back on this time in my life, I see that it was a preparation for positive things to come.

Giant Forest Lodge is one of the two main areas where the sequoia trees are found. We rented rustic cabins. Laura and I had one; most of the other women had decided to pitch their tents at another location and slept by a beautiful stream in a flower-strewn meadow. We had come to the sequoias three days before the fall equinox, a very powerful time when one is communing with Mother Earth. I didn't know that at the time either.

Each day, Sandy took us as a group to specific sites where sequoia trees grew, and we would meditate as a group for about half an hour, then journal our experiences and move on to the next location. We were meditating four times daily, and after the first day I was so spacy and out of my body that I walked around as though I were drunk! I might add that the other women had decided to fast during this five-day spiritual quest. I, on the other hand, because I had hypoglycemia, couldn't miss a meal or I was in deep trouble. So I was over at the lodge cafeteria eating food — including meat.

Laura got in trouble on the second day of the fast and decided to start eating meals, too. Sandy scorned us for eating. I got a little upset with her admonishment, because intuitively I knew that it didn't matter what we did or did not eat. If something "spiritual" was supposed to happen to us, it would, regardless. Sandy disagreed with me. I told her that she had a choice: either tell me I couldn't continue meditating with the group because I was eating three meals a day, or ask me to leave the group altogether. She decided to let Laura and me stay, even though we were looked down upon for eating.

After the second day I was so spaced out that I told Sandy that the most I was going to meditate was twice a day, not four times a day.

She didn't like my decision, but I was becoming so "thinned out" by the meditation that I was too spacy for my own good. I had to respect what my body could take and not try to keep up with the other ladies, who seemed perfectly in tune with the heavy meditation schedule.

Every evening we would meet out on Beetle Rock, a huge smooth, gray-black slab of lava rock that faced west, and we would meditate and pray. I had an incredible vision on the second evening. I saw a beautiful angel of great power come out of the west and he touched each one of us on the head. I saw a flame leaping from our crown chakras as he touched each one of us with his sword. I was amazed and deeply moved by this vision. When the Sun had set and we had journaled, it was normal for all of us to tell what had happened – if anything.

THE REALITY OF A VISION

I was the last to tell my experience, and Sandy was aghast when I finished describing what I had seen. She asked me if I knew who had come to us. Being Cherokee-raised, I wasn't into Christian dogma at all, and I said no. The group just shook their heads and looked at me as though I were crazy. Sandy excitedly said that I'd seen Michael, the archangel. They were very impressed with this, but I wasn't the least touched by it. Angels weren't in my reality, my vocabulary or my existence. I wasn't impressed at all, but I knew the vision had been real; it had actually happened. Sandy said Michael had given each of us a gift by opening up our crown chakras with the sacred fire of the Holy Ghost.

I didn't relate too well to that, but I honored her spiritual affiliation. My sense of it was that angels were symbolic, and I respected any symbolism. It was just for me to figure out how an angel fit into my reality. It wasn't until many, many years later that Michael came back into my life in his angelic form and then I understood why he'd visited me back then. When he returned the second time I was not resistant, as I had been, and I understood the crossover connection and how it fit beautifully into my Red Road experience.

The next morning, we went to our original meditation point, a place where three sequoia trees had grown together and formed a fantastic place within them where seven women could sit, legs crossed, and meditate. With every meditation I was feeling so thinned out, so not-of-this-world, that it was incredible. We trekked to our next site, where five sequoias towered. I was drawn like a magnet to one sequoia, and I sat down with my back against his smooth, strong trunk.

KNOWING WHETHER OR NOT YOU'RE IN THE RIGHT PLACE

I closed my eyes and heard the other women all choosing where they would sit to meditate. One of the women came over to the sequoia where I was sitting and I opened my eyes briefly. I got an overpowering sense that this sequoia didn't want her sitting by him. Instantly, I saw a bee rise from the pine needles right in front of my feet and attack her. She yelped and leaned back.

"I guess I'm not supposed to sit there," she said.

I shrugged. It wasn't my decision to make.

She pointed to the ground in front of my feet, her eyes widening tremendously. "Oh, my God, look. That's a nest of ground bees in front of your feet! You're going to get stung! You shouldn't sit next to this tree."

I saw the nest at that moment — not more than six inches from my shoes. I shrugged again. "It's going to be okay," I said. "The bees will leave me alone." And I knew they would — I just felt it instinctively.

The woman shrugged. "You're going to get stung if you aren't careful." She walked away to a "safer" tree and sat down with one of the other women.

I knew the bees wouldn't bother me. I knew I was in the right place. I closed my eyes and almost instantly, I felt the living spirit within the sequoia. I felt his "arms" come around me, gently, as if to embrace me lovingly. At that moment I saw an incredible green light come out from around him and begin to spiral around me and his trunk. The green light moved up to the top of the tree. I felt myself melting into the center of the sequoia. It was an odd sensation. I felt myself moving through the bark, the cambium and the wood of the tree. As I moved into the center of the tree, I was surrounded by powerful golden light moving like a river downward, being pumped in huge volumes through the tree and into its roots.

At that moment, I saw a large green man, the spirit of the tree, materialize next to me. He didn't have much of a shape — vaguely human, but no face, just a bright apple-green plasma. He told me his name and he welcomed me. I was amazed because I was there in every way. I no longer heard any external noise from the ladies, from the birds singing. I was no longer in my body at all. I couldn't feel the bark against my back or the tickle of the pine needles against my bare legs.

I thanked Talal (not his real name) for allowing me to come into him, to see what he did. I felt him smile and he said, "Come with me. I want to show you where you come from." Intrigued, I said I'd go. Talal gently wrapped his "hand" around my arm and I felt myself flying upward through the core of the sequoia in that stream of incredibly powerful and beautiful golden light coursing down through it. I felt us break free of the tree branches, I saw my sisters down below, meditating, and I looked up. I saw a beautiful golden light, like a gold ribbon, flowing through the bright blue sky. Talal took me on a swift journey up and out of the stratosphere, up beyond Mother Earth and out into space. The gold ribbon went through the star systems, through galaxies, and I saw it all, amazed.

Finally, the gold road came to an end, and my mouth hung open in amazement. The gold road spread out like fine, delicate filigree into an oval basket shape. Up above this "basket" of gold energy was a huge, golden egg. It was so large that we looked like a pair of ants hovering above it.

"This is where you come from," Talal said, pointing to the golden egg.

I was speechless. I felt the incredible energy, the love, emanating from this opaque golden egg. "What's inside it?"

SEQUOIAS TRANSMIT COSMIC ENERGY

I felt Talal smile. "You will be shown what is inside when the time is appropriate. Would you like to see where this energy goes?"

"Sure," I said. We went back onto the path of gold light, back into the stratosphere, back into the tree and followed this gold energy down into the root system of the sequoia. This tremendous pumping of energy was leaving the roots of the sequoias and being given to Mother Earth. Talal explained that the sequoia trees act as transmitters for this energy that comes from the cosmos, and that this energy feeds Mother Earth. Without these trees pumping this energy, Mother Earth would die.

Talal brought me out of the roots and back into the center of himself, where the gold light rushed all around us. I thanked him. He told me that he'd like to work with me and I said yes, shaken and humbled. I hadn't known trees had these powerful spirits in them.

I'd known that they had spirits, but not to this degree. He embraced me and I felt such love from him that I cried. He told me it was time to go back, that the women were coming out of their meditations. I didn't want to go, but he told me I must—and that he'd be there for me anytime I called his name.

I felt myself moving from the center of the sequoia, out through the wood and bark and back into my body. Tears were running down my face as I returned to my body. Everyone else had already come out of meditation and were quietly writing in their journals. I was so shaken and touched by the experience that it was tough to write, to be coherent. Finally, I told the group about the experience, omitting the sequoia's name.

I felt an incredible peace within me that rest of the day, and I decided not to do any more meditation with the group because I understood that I had come to receive this vision.

Interestingly enough, the woman who had wanted to sit with me and Talal sneaked back to him the next day. That evening she came back angry and accusing. She confronted me and told me that she'd gone back to meditate with Talal. When she'd sat down against him, the ground bees had attacked her and they'd stung her all over her legs, driving her away from Talal and out of the area. She accused me of doing it!

NEGATIVITY PRODUCES NOTHING

I was amazed and hurt by her accusation. I told her I had nothing to do with it. The next morning, I trekked out to Talal and sat down—with his permission—and went into an altered state. I asked him about this woman and her getting stung. Since the vision, I'd been feeling an incredible, conscious link with Talal. I felt his smile and he told me that the woman was jealous of my experience and wanted one of her own, so she'd come up to him demanding it. Talal told me that he'd asked the Bee People to drive her away since he couldn't. She had come to him with a negative heart and a negative reason, so he wanted nothing to do with her.

TREE PEOPLE

Talal has taught me much about the Tree People, about the powerful devas who reside within the largest and oldest trees of the world. They are very powerful "people" in their own right. He's been with me ever since and was responsible for healing Molly, my

Arabian mare who had colic and nearly died of it until I asked him for his help.

Every once in a while, I go back to see Talal physically. But he is with me everywhere and will pop into my conscious awareness from time to time.

My ability to speak with the Tree People has been in place ever since. I'm convinced that this particular vision and the melding with this tree deva has helped me to come back into my feminine energy. Why? Because all trees nurture. It's true the giant sequoias, the largest trees in the world, have a special task of "feeding" Mother Earth cosmic energy to help her to stay well. But every tree is like a radio antenna bringing in cosmic food for her, too — just on a smaller scale.

If you are drawn to a particular tree, go give it a gift of food — not money. And not meat. I was taught by Talal that no one should automatically think that every tree wants a human being for a friend, for they do not. Humans have been responsible for more damage to the Tree Nation than any other single cause. And trees, I found out, are just like people in that they have very singular, individual personalities. There are trees who are highly evolved, like some humans, and there are others who are just starting on a very primitive level, like other humans.

The best way to see if a tree wants your attention, your love, your care, is to approach it with a gift of food. Or, your intent. Either is appropriate. Stand there and mentally ask the tree if it's okay if you sit down and meditate with it. You'll receive a feeling. If it feels positive, go sit down. If it does not, move on and ask another tree until you find one that is welcoming you.

It's important not to expect anything. When I went on my sequoia trek, I expected nothing at all — and look what happened. Take a journal with you and write down any feelings, thoughts, symbols or things that happen to you when you meditate with your tree partner. Sooner or later, the spirit of the tree will "knock at your door," but it will be on the tree spirit's time, not yours. So many tree spirits are wary of humans, that you might have to prove your intent again and again by coming with a gift, sitting down and meditating, showing your integrity toward the tree spirit. Don't give up! If you are meant to truly get in touch with the spirit of the tree, it will happen.

Once the bond is in place, the tree spirit is with you forever. It's a marriage of sorts, for it is a bond of trust and love. To see this in another perspective, working with the devas and their kingdoms when we're from another kingdom creates the crossover experiences — balance, if you will — that can come into being when you are touching and working with the trees.

Once the contact is made, you have a wonderful lifelong relationship.

Horse Medicine, Part 1

Every person has "medicine" — talents, skills and abilities. In the Native American vernacular, *medicine* means that you are capable and have knowledge in a specific area. It's used in another way, too. We believe that our brothers and sisters (all living things) are our teachers. We don't take an arrogant view and look down upon them. On the contrary, we consider ourselves part of the fabric, the whole, of life. One human being is not better or smarter than a tree, a wolf or a rock. A human being has certain skills just as a tree, a wolf or a rock has. Whether humanity recognizes, honors or respects the skills of the tree, wolf or rock is another thing.

I have a saying: Whatever you're drawn to, whatever you love, is your medicine. Having a medicine doesn't necessarily mean you'll be good at it at first. Remember that in a previous chapter I told you that if something visits you three times, either in a dream or in reality, it is an invitation to take the medicine? Well, that's true.

Taking a medicine means we've consciously (or sometimes unconsciously) chosen to put ourselves on a particular path of learning.

If the recipient takes the medicine in a humble way, then she will learn a great deal. However, grabbing a medicine without respect means not much will come out of such a one-sided relationship.

Everyone has a memory of the very first medicine she/he was given or invited to take. Usually it happens in childhood. I want to share with you my first medicine in the hope that it will make you think back to the time when it happened to you. The questions you want to ask yourself about your first medicine are: Have I learned everything I can from it? Have I become it? How? What skills or teaching did I learn and then incorporate into the fabric of my every-day life? Let me give you an example.

When I was three years old my parents put me on a very large horse. I was absolutely paralyzed with fear of this huge animal. But my parents knew something I didn't — that horse medicine was going to play a very important part in my development as a teenager. So my first run-in with a horse wasn't very positive and, as a matter of fact, that is my first memory — sitting in that saddle, squalling like a cat, as frightened as I could be.

Somehow the experience must not have been quite as negative as I would think it would have been. I can remember that when I was five I had a "stick horse" I rode around on, hour after hour. One time, a breathtakingly beautiful, pure white horse got loose and ran right in front of me as I was playing. He was large, heavily muscled with no halter — just running wild and free. I remember coming slowly out of the crouched position in which I had been playing mar-bles in the dirt. My mouth fell open and my eyes grew huge as this magnificent animal entered my vision and my world.

I have never forgotten that white horse. It was as if he had been placed in my path to remind me of my first medicine: the horse. Of course, I wasn't cognizant that this was happening at the time, even though it was significant. That horse is forever branded in my mem-ory, even to this day. To me, he symbolized wild, uninhibited free-dom, the wind blowing his long, thick mane, his tail arched, the strands flowing like high cirrus clouds. His nostrils were flared, his eyes dark and intelligent. I remember that he halted in front of me, looking at me intently. Then, lifting his tail, he galloped off.

From that time on, I became "horse-crazy." From a Native American perspective I would say that the horse brought his medi-cine to me, gifted me and I accepted it, albeit on an unconscious level. How horse-crazy was I? I began to try to draw them at a very early age — and they were pitiful attempts at first. But by the time I was nine years old, I was quite an artist. (As a matter of fact, it led directly to my getting a degree in commercial art later on.) The driving need to draw horses, to capture their wild, unfettered beauty, their power and boldness, made me draw until my fingers ached.

I also collected plastic horses, although we were so poor that I went around collecting pop bottles to get enough money to buy just one — a beautiful palomino with a sun-gold body and a flowing white mane. I worked diligently for a year, collecting bottles and saving the money until I could proudly make my purchase at a local drugstore. Buying my one and only plastic horse was a thrill I will never forget.

That year when I was nine taught me about patience, working hard and saving money to get something I wanted. It is a lesson I carry with me to this day. I know that if I work hard and put forth my best effort (even if I sometimes fail or don't do as well as someone else), that I will get the reward I'm seeking — and I always do. So, horse medicine had given me two great life lessons: first, that I had artistic skills and, second, that with hard work, a goal could be achieved. It's pretty good for a medicine to impart such powerful, long-lasting lessons!

By the time I was thirteen, I wanted a horse so badly I could taste it. So I rounded up my other siblings and came up with a grand way to get the money to buy a horse. I would draw pictures of horses on sheets of typewriter paper and they would go around the neighborhood selling them for five cents a piece! Everyone thought that was a great idea, so I churned out hundreds of pictures that very understanding (and, I'm sure, amused) neighbors bought. I ended up with twenty-five dollars in proceeds.

That same year when we were living in Blackfoot, Idaho, because we were so poor (my parents would never have thought of taking welfare), we decided the whole family should pick potatoes — seven cents for a one hundred-pound sack. Idaho is big potato country, and in three weeks, I had made forty-five dollars! That was a huge amount to me, and the horse sure looked in reach.

We moved again, this time to Klamath Falls, Oregon, and all the money the entire family had made picking potatoes had to be used to get us to Oregon. I was devastated in one way, but I also felt proud that my forty-five dollars could help the family as a whole. I knew that somehow, once we reached Oregon, I would find a way to make money again and buy that horse.

When I was fourteen, fate intervened. One day I was reading the classified ads in the newspaper and saw this ad: "Horses for sale." Something grabbed me and I picked up the phone and called. Mr. Soder (I'll never forget his name) answered. He said he had a bunch of wild mustangs over at the livestock yard that were going to be slaughtered if they weren't bought in the next couple days. I panicked. Somehow I knew my horse was in that bunch. I asked him what he had to sell. He told me about a two-year-old sorrel mustang stallion, and I got really excited. I knew this was the horse! My stomach clenched as I whispered, "How much do you want for him?"

"Forty-five dollars."

My heart sank. That was the exact amount I had earned in Idaho and had anticipated using to buy a horse. I knew the family was in dire straits financially, and I knew we didn't have an extra forty-five dollars. Completely devastated, I quietly thanked him and hung up. But I didn't give up. I kept trying to think of a way to buy the horse. I hit upon an idea and excitedly called back Mr. Soder. I asked him if he'd take my bicycle, which had cost fifty dollars new (four years before), in trade for the stallion. He laughed in a kindly sort of way and said he was sorry, he couldn't.

I was dreadfully disappointed. I was morose and depressed. When my parents got home, my mother noticed my glum attitude. At the dinner table she asked me what was wrong. I was so distraught that I sat there and told them. Then I cried. I felt awful that I was making them miserable. I couldn't bear the thought that I was going to lose this stallion to chicken feed. I saw the compassion in my parents' eyes. My father said, "Forty-five dollars is a lot of money."

"I know," I said, sniffling. "Too much. I know we don't have it."

Nothing more was said at the dinner table, and I didn't eat much at all. My stomach was tied in a knot of grief. In my heart, I'd already found a name for my two-year-old stallion — Pretty Boy. I could see him visually in my forehead when I closed my eyes, and for the rest of the evening, I felt totally empty.

The next evening at the dinner table, my father cleared his throat. "We're going to let you buy that horse."

I gasped, my fork falling to my plate. "What?"

Mom smiled gently. "You remember that forty-five dollars you made picking potatoes that we had to use to move here?"

"Yes," I gulped, my mouth still hanging open.

Her smile increased and she looked at my father. "Well, we've decided that since you loaned us that amount, we can pay it back by getting you this horse. Is that all right?"

Was it ever! I said yes and was immediately on the phone to Mr. Soder, who then talked to my father. The stallion would be delivered to our home the next day!

In the next chapter I want to continue to share what horse medicine has done for me. I'm sure everyone has a similar story. We're constantly getting offers for new medicine to add to that which we've already perfected and are using. New medicine is about continued growth on all levels, including spirituality. But certain medicines are foundations and they will carry us through life. I want to share how much horse medicine has been a part of mine.

Horse Medicine, Part 2

I mentioned in the previous chapter that at the age of nine, I was completely horse-crazy. I wanted one so badly, and I kept drawing horses and dreaming of owning one some day. I knew that because we were so poor, I'd never be able to have one. So I focused with nine-year-old ferocity on the next best thing: a plastic horse from the local drugstore in Ontario, Oregon.

I used to stand there and salivate, dreaming and looking at that beautiful plastic palomino horse with the western saddle. The price was $2.50 – an incredibly large sum to me. Understand that it took walking the mile-long dirt road in front of our house to find enough pop bottles just to buy a cherished candy bar once a week.

There was no such thing as an allowance at our house. Indeed, my father hunted regularly just to put food on the table, and we ate a lot of cottontail rabbit, catfish and deer. We couldn't even afford 29 cent-a-pound hamburger for our family of five, such was our financial worth.

I added up five cents a week of found pop bottles to figure out how long it would take to buy that plastic palomino horse in the drugstore window. It would take 25 weeks! That was a terribly long amount of time in my small world, and I literally had a gnawing ache in my stomach because of wanting that horse so badly.

As fate would have it, my horse medicine was working on me big-time, although I never realized it then. In our family we were taught never to lie, cheat or steal. Those were family values no one dared to cross.

My parents were broad-minded and encouraged the three of us children to go to any church we wished to attend. They weren't Christian, but they honored all religions — Buddhist, Moslem, Christian and pagan. They wanted us to go to learn about people, about other ways of living and other religions, feeling this was important to us — and it was.

At the time we were going to the Church of the Nazarene. I had a perfect attendance record for one year, never having missed Sunday school. Mom would always join us for the service after Sunday school, and the four of us would sit there and listen to Reverend Wilson. I liked Reverend Wilson. He was about six feet tall, and he always looked splendid and impressive in a dark blue pinstripe suit. He had bulldog jowls but kindly blue eyes and always a wonderful smile. He loved kids and I always loved being hugged by him when he was saying good-bye to the parishioners at the front of the church as we left after his services.

One particular Sunday as we sat listening to the sermon, Reverend Wilson stopped and announced that there was going to be a contest among the Sunday school attendees. Whoever could get the most kids to come with him/her to attend the next week's Sunday school would get — my eyes popped out of my head as the reverend drew a beautiful plastic pinto horse from behind his podium and held it up for all to see. It was the most impressive, awe-inspiring plastic horse I'd ever seen.

My heart began to race. I began to fight. My mind was galloping along. I wanted that horse. It was mine! Mine! I looked around, scowling. I saw how many other kids were inspired and excited as they, too, looked at that splendid plastic horse. I clenched my fist. No one could have it but me. It was mine, I just knew it. I was desperate, and during the school week, I got four kids to volunteer to come. In my heart, I knew four might not be enough, and the need for that plastic horse was so great that I was worried.

Finally, after the Sunday sermon, Reverend Wilson asked all of us who had brought our friends to Sunday school to stand up and report how many children we'd brought. I heard one, two, three and, even worse, Sarah had four —just like me! I went into a spasm of absolute grief and anguish. I had four, too. I was sweating. My heart was pounding like a sledge-hammer. Reverend Wilson was holding up that plastic pinto horse. It was so shiny, so dark brown with dramatic white spots. I froze with need.

I was the last child to report my figures. Sarah had brought four friends, but no one else rivaled that number. Reverend Wilson looked at me with a kindly expression and asked how many I'd brought. In that moment, my throat closed and I stopped breathing. I held my breath. When I let it out, I said, "Five."

It was a bald lie. A terrible lie. The next few minutes were a blur to me as everyone broke out in applause — and the church was filled with over one hundred parishioners. I remember feeling heat flooding my face as I stumbled past my siblings and mother to get to the end of the pew. Reverend Wilson was smiling grandly, holding out the plastic horse to me. Me! Somehow, I put the shame of my lie aside as my gaze fixed on the horse. Oh, how I'd wanted it so badly, and now the pinto horse was mine. Mine! The reverend patted my shoulder fondly and handed me the horse. Then he turned me around to face the parishioners and asked everyone to give me a big hand.

All I can remember from that awful, gut-churning moment was my hands clutching the pinto horse so hard that my fingers ached and my knuckles hurt. No one was going to take this horse away from me. No one. As I stumbled in a daze back to the pew where my family was sitting, I was patted on the shoulder, congratulated and smiled at endlessly. I felt shame so devastating that all I could do was hang my head and hurry to my seat.

On the way home my sister began to badger me.

"How many friends did you say you got to come?"

"Five," I muttered, still clutching that horse, still staring at it, disbelieving that it was really mine.

"Who are they?"

I was irritated. My sister and I had never gotten along, and just then I hated her curiosity. "You wouldn't know them!" I shot back. I saw my mother glance at me as she drove. Sweat popped out on my upper lip.

"Sure I would! We go to the same school. We're only a grade apart. Who are they?"

By this time I wanted to turn around and hit her right in the mouth, such was my desperation over the chance of being found out. My voice wobbled, not with anger but with fear, as I reeled off the first four names. And then—I made up a fifth name.

My sister frowned. "I don't know any Jenny Smith."

"I told you, you wouldn't know all of them!" I snapped back.

My mother turned and looked at me, frowning.

Oh no, I thought. She knows I'm lying! My mother was and still is a highly intuitive person. My stomach flip-flopped, my heart was thudding like a runaway freight train and my palms grew sweaty. The horse slipped in my hands.

"Who is this Jenny Smith?" Mom asked.

I bit down hard on my lower lip and closed my eyes. I didn't want to lie again. I realized in a terrible rush that one lie had to be covered by other lies, just to keep the story going. I didn't have much practice at lying, so I sat there speechless. I refused to lie to my mother. I'd lie to my sister but not to her.

My mother sighed. "We'll talk of this when we get home."

"I thought so," my sister cried triumphantly. "She lied! There wasn't any fifth person. You lied!"

By now, I was melting into a pool of humiliation, shame and perspiration. As I stared down at the horse, I realized that my mother was going to take it away from me. I also realized I had it coming. That lie was a terrible thing, and I looked through my lashes at my mother's set features. She looked upset. That hurt worse than anything because I loved my mother with a fierceness that defied description, and I'd never do anything to make her upset or angry with me.

Once home, clutching my plastic horse, I morosely followed my mother into the kitchen, where she turned and confronted me. My sister and brother were standing in the entrance, waiting.

"Well, did you lie?" my mother asked me.

I stood there, tears welling up in my eyes. I kept turning the horse nervously between my sweaty hands.

"Did you?" She leaned down and placed her hands on her lips, her hazel eyes drilling into my blue ones.

"I—I . . . ," I choked and then sobbed a little. I tried to get hold of myself. "Y-yes," I whispered, and then broke into a gale of tears.

"How could you!" my mother said. She threw her hands up and paced the kitchen. "How could you?"

Her words hurt me so much that I just stood there sniffling, sobbing and still clutching that plastic horse.

"What's worst," she said, coming back over to me, "is that you not only lied to a minister, you lied in front of the whole congregation!"

Wiping my runny nose, I looked up at her. "I'm sorry. I-I just wanted the horse, that was all."

"You don't ever lie to get anything! Not ever!" She took the horse out of my hands.

I didn't even try to stop her from taking the horse. I knew it was just punishment. The worst part was that I was hurting because it was the first time I'd ever lied to my mother. The wounded look on her face just sent me into more tears and sobs. I hadn't meant to hurt her, but in my greed to get the plastic horse, I'd done the unthinkable.

"I'm going to call Reverend Wilson right now."

I stood motionless as she made the call to his home. My mother explained everything, apologizing a number of times. Finally, I heard her say, "Yes, we're coming right over and she will give the horse back to you."

I cried harder. Not only had I hurt my mother, I was losing the one thing in the world I wanted more than anything else. As I dragged out of the kitchen, following my mother to the car, my sister smirked at me.

"See? You don't lie and get away with it."

I was too miserable to be angry with her. I knew I deserved whatever I got. Further, my mother told me I was not only going to have to give the horse back, but I'd also have to apologize directly to Reverend Wilson. I was shocked and dismayed. I liked Reverend Wilson, and I was sort of afraid of him because he was such an important man in Ontario. All I could do was sit in the front seat, my hands empty, eyes swollen and red with tears running down my cheeks. I'd never felt so miserable in my life.

Reverend Wilson and his wife met us at the door. They were gracious and invited us inside. I was agog at the rich furnishings in their home. It was like a palace compared to ours. As we were ushered into the living room, I couldn't bear to look at anyone. My mother and I faced them. She gave me the horse.

Choking, I whispered as I looked up at Reverend Wilson, "I lied this morning, and I feel *so* bad about it." I sniffed. More tears fell. I thrust out the beautiful brown-and-white pinto horse to him. "H-here, this is yours. It belongs to Sarah, not me. I only got four kids to come, not five. I lied." I struggled to meet his eyes. "I'm really sorry." And I was, in the most abject, humiliated and humble of ways.

I was surprised as I saw Reverend Wilson's face turn so very kind and compassionate. I'd never seen his eyes look so warm, so filled with love as they did when he took the horse.

"You had the courage to come back and tell me about your lie," he told me gently. "God will forgive a person who owns up to a lie."

"I-I'll never lie again," I sobbed. "I'm sorry, so sorry."

Reverend Wilson put his hand on my shoulder. "It's going to be all right."

My mother said in a stern voice, "You give that horse to Sarah, Reverend."

"But," he protested, patting my shoulder, "it was a tie."

I could see how distraught Reverend Wilson was over my crying, but I just couldn't help it. I'd never cried in front of strangers before, and certainly not in front of someone like Reverend Wilson. I had always cried alone.

"Give it to Sarah."

Reverend Wilson shrugged. He gave me his linen handkerchief to dry my eyes and blow my nose.

"Under the circumstances, couldn't we just let your daughter keep the horse? I can see how much it means to her. Sarah will never know, and the fact that she came and told me about the lie is enough punishment."

My heart raced as I heard Reverend Wilson's words. I looked up, astonished. He was holding the pinto horse out to me.

"She won't learn her lesson if you give it back to her."

The words chilled me as my mother spoke them. In my heart, I knew that wasn't true. I looked longingly at the horse. I saw the reverend hesitate.

"She's right," Reverend Wilson's wife added softly, patting her husband's arm comfortingly. "We'll let Sarah have it."

I stood there, knowing I didn't deserve the horse. I knew my mother was right. I was so numb with grief and shame that all I wanted to do was go home, go to the attic where our beds were and hide.

On the way home, there was nothing but silence in the car. I felt better, if the truth be known, because now it was over. I didn't have to lie any more to cover up the first lies. My mother reached over and gently touched my head.

"Why don't you think of ways to buy that plastic horse at the drugstore? You can find pop bottles alongside the road."

I nodded. "Yes . . . I will."

"It's better to earn something the right way," my mother said. She smiled slightly at me.

Despite everything, I knew my mother had never stopped loving me. It was such a wonderful realization, that all the shame and humiliation lifted. But the lesson about lying never did. I've never wanted anything quite so badly since that fateful day. But what I did want, I knew without a doubt, I'd have to earn honestly and with hard work.

Over the next 25 weeks, I earned the money to buy that palomino horse from the drugstore. I proudly marched into that store with my mother with the $2.50 in my small hands. I plopped it down on the counter. I asked for the horse, and the woman smiled and got it out of the display window for me.

"That will be $2.56," she said.

I was crestfallen. I hadn't counted on tax. For one agonizing moment, I knew the horse was going to be taken from me again. I'd have to wait two weeks longer and find more pop bottles to make the necessary money.

"I'll get the tax," my mother said.

Turning, I gasped, "You will?"

She dug into her beat-up, old leather purse. "I wish I could do more, honey."

It was enough. More than enough. As my mother put the nickel and penny on the counter, I realized with a rush of joy that the horse was mine — earned the right way, this time. With that palomino horse in hand, I think I floated out of that drugstore.

Horse medicine has taught me a great deal about being myself, and about accepting myself for what I am and am not, for horses never put on airs, either. Horses have taught me about personal freedom, a freedom that is found on the inner planes of ourselves. And most of all, horses have taught me not to lie — *ever!*

Hummingbird Medicine

The other day I was out in our rose garden, sitting on the bench in the early morning hours. It was about 5 a.m. I had a cup of coffee in my hands and I was sitting down to rest for a moment after turning on the sprinkler in the rose garden. In Arizona desert country, one does not water a garden or do any hard physical work except in the early morning hours or near dusk. The heat of the day is just too intense for humans and animals alike.

The droplets of water shimmered in a profusion of rainbow colors as Father Sun edged over the wall of our black basalt and red sandstone canyon. The roses, some forty in all, in both tree and bush forms, were heavy with flowers. The fragrance was heady and I inhaled it deeply into my lungs.

I closed my eyes. Then I heard the thrum of a hummingbird whizzing by me at high speed. I looked around, my ears tracing the sound. I saw a small gray female hummingbird with some streaks of iridescent green along her body near a rose bush not ten feet away.

There was one huge rose, pink with yellow in the center, that was heavy with droplets of water. At first the female hummingbird dipped daintily around it, sipping water off the leaves where the droplets had pearled. Then, to my great surprise, she landed in the center of the rose, which was five times larger than she was, and began to take a bath!

I watched, fascinated, having never thought of a rose as a bathtub. But obviously she had. I marveled at the hummingbird's innate creativity, her practicality, in unthinkingly turning a simple thing into something usable. Who would ever have thought that a rose would be a convenient bird bath? I sat there laughing out loud, delighted with the hummingbird's intelligence. She splashed this way and that, her tiny, thin wings sending little showers of water over the edges of the petals and onto the green grass below.

I remembered times when I had taken a rose-scented bubble bath, but this hummingbird had the best of all worlds. She had a real rose with its wonderful fragrance, she had the water and she had her "tub" – all natural. Again, I was in awe of hummingbirds. But then, I always have been.

The South American Indians have always held the hummingbird in high esteem, even above the hawks and eagles. Only of late have the North American Indians caught on to this fabulous little midget of the feathered world and her enormous powers. Most Native Americans revere eagle medicine and then hawk medicine – but nothing as small or "wimpy" as a hummingbird!

When I started my training with Sam, my Cherokee teacher, I noticed hummingbirds would dive-bomb me or wing past me at a high rate of speed, sounding like miniature thunder, always startling me, always catching me off guard. I asked him about this one time.

"I dunno. What do you feel about it?" He squinted, the Sun against his eyes, the battered old, white straw cowboy hat jammed down on his head.

I groaned. "Here we go again," and then I smiled because by this time, I was very much aware of Sam's teaching methods which were actually a way of getting me in touch with my own experience, observation, intuition and feelings.

His mouth pulled into a semblance of a one-cornered grin. He took the red handkerchief he had around his neck and slowly untied it. "Hummers are real special."

"Yeah?"

He smiled and wiped his neck and cheeks and then removed his hat to swab down his perspiring brow. "You tell me."

Sam always saw through my games of trying to squeeze even a bit of an answer out of him. I looked down into the shade of a pin oak. We were high above Los Angeles, up in the yellowed grass hills that were dry with summer heat. I picked at a dead foxtail between my crossed legs.

"I don't know much about hummers," I lamented.

"Not many Indians do."

"Well," I said a little defiantly, "it isn't as though hummers are indigenous to North America."

"Oh, but they are. Every spring through fall they come north." Sam made a gesture to the north and east. "They are found everywhere, but Indians don't pay much attention to them." He scowled. "And that's too bad."

I felt a thrill of excitement go through me as I watched Sam sitting across from me on a big flat rock. He nudged the cowboy hat a bit off his brow, his eyes trained on the thick dark blanket of pollution that always embraced Los Angeles.

Frantically, I searched my mind for any information I could recall on hummers. "They're rainbow colored!" I felt pleased with my observation.

"That's true. So are macaws, peacocks and parrots."

Now it was my turn to scowl. Okay, back to the drawing board. "Colors do mean something," I muttered defiantly.

"No argument there. What else?" he prodded, his dark eyes settling on me.

I hated it when Sam watched me. I knew he was clairvoyant, that he could see not only me but also my aura, and Great Spirit knew what else. I trailed my finger in the dry white dust.

"They drink nectar for food, I think. They can't even eat bugs."

"So?"

My mouth drew itself in, and I felt an internal desperation. I shrugged. "On a symbolic level, would that make them sweet?"

"In what sense of the word?"

"I knew you were going to ask that." Damn! I squirmed and then squirmed some more, thinking.

"It's common knowledge that vegetarians of any kind are usually less aggressive and warlike than those of their kin who eat meat," Sam drawled, picking a foxtail and placing it in the corner of his mouth.   "Meat-eaters just tend to be warriors, to be aggressive instead of maybe compromising."

"So hummingbird medicine would be passive?" I asked, grasping literally at straws.

"What do you think?"

"I would think so."

"Hummers aren't passive. That's not the right word you're lookin' for."

I scratched my head. "Friendly?"

"Maybe." He smiled briefly. "Why don't you go do some research on hummers and we'll talk more after that?"

I did just that. I went to my local library and searched through a lot of different books, writing up all the characteristics of hummers. The next time I saw Sam, I arrived with a bunch of paper covered with notes.

"I think the neatest thing the hummer can do and that no other bird in the world can do is to fly in any direction," I told Sam proudly, waving the papers at him.

"How could you use that in the context of our world?"

I stopped, completely stymied. I saw the glint in Sam's eyes and I knew he was pleased with my research, but as usual he was going to force me to stretch myself in all kinds of directions.

"There are days when I feel like a hummer," I told him in a grumbling tone.

"Oh?"

"Yeah, you make me stretch, pull, turn myself into a pretzel and knot myself up trying to give you the right answers!"

He laughed long and loud, slapping his weathered, dark brown hands against his knees. Wiping the tears from the corners of his eyes, he settled his gaze on me.

"That was a good answer," he praised.

I colored beneath his sincerity, and I saw the gleam of pride in his eyes. "Thanks, I guess."

"I guess I'm just going to have to drag you kicking and screaming into hummer medicine," he said jovially. Sam sat on a picnic bench, his hat in his hands. We were sitting in the back yard of his home.

"I guess you are. So how does the hummer's ability to fly in all directions apply to us?"

"Great question. What's the answer?"

"If I had one, don't you think I'd be giving it to you?"

Chuckling, Sam put the hat on his head. "What profession among our people would require hummer medicine?"

I screwed up my brow in thought. Finally, after about five minutes, I said, "I give up. What?"

"Shamans. Not medicine people but shamans."

My eyes widened. "Shamans?"

"Sure. They differ from medicine people in a lot of ways. Their skill is in zipping in and out of other dimensions. Medicine people can't do that."

The lights suddenly went on for me and I snapped my fingers. "Hummer medicine is shaman's medicine!"

"Exactly." Sam smiled a little and folded his hands in front of him on the redwood table. "Shamanism is the only trade I know of in which you *have* to be in two places simultaneously. The hummer can change direction at will, so fast that it is almost in two places simultaneously. That's why the South American Indians hold the hummer more sacred than eagles and hawks. The hummer is the only bird able to fly forward, sideways and in reverse. A shaman has to do similar things when she or he is in a journeying state. Isn't that true?"

It didn't take me long to agree to that. "So someone who is able to move interdimensionally would have hummer medicine?"

"Yes. And if they don't, they aren't very good at what they say they do," Sam said with a little smile. "Your good shamans always have hummer medicine."

I knew from my own experience that in an altered state induced by a drumbeat, I was literally in two places at once. My left brain was aware of the noises of the third dimension. My right brain allowed me the entrance into and the viewing of all the invisible dimensions that interpenetrate and surround us — simultaneously. I could zip, like a hummer, into the light world, the dark world or the real world, wherever my guides took me to retrieve pieces of soul for a person.

"Is that why hummers have been dive-bombing me?" I asked dryly.

"You got it," Sam congratulated. "So why don't you go make an offering to the Hummingbird People. Tell them you accept their medicine and ask them to continue to be your teachers."

Blushing sheepishly, I nodded. "Nothing like hitting me over the head with a two-by-four, is it?"

He laughed and eased off the bench. "It's okay. The Hummer People have infinite patience."

Good thing, I thought as I walked with Sam through his house to my car, which was parked along the curb. It was one thing to be blind, deaf and dumb but another to be just plain unaware – and I'd been unaware. I'd made the fatal mistake of pooh-poohing hummer medicine as meaningless because the bird was small. Further, it was the equal of the mighty eagle or hawk, lacking not only size but also aggressiveness. I had a lot to take stock of regarding myself because of this unfolding awareness about hummer medicine. I was a shaman-in-training, and I wasn't very pleased with my prejudice.

Hummer medicine has taught me a great deal. One of the great things about hummingbirds is that they never get pushy – except at the feeding station, where males will dive-bomb one another to "claim territory." Have you ever watched a hummer getting nectar from a flower? It's a dance, a beautiful, gentle dance. There's nothing aggressive about hummers; they are just steady and patient in getting the nectar from the flower they've chosen, no matter how many times they have to go back to do it and get it "right."

Hummers have taught me patience regarding myself and projects and in regard to myself and other people. I've learned to have patience with people in a way that I never had before. And where my assertiveness always used to prevail, I've learned how to approach an individual or situation more gently, without being a bull in a china shop but still with firmness. So the hummers have taught me something I desperately needed to learn – which had nothing to do with shamanism, but which I had to learn in order to become a better human being.

I see hummers as being the diplomats of life, too. I'm not a very diplomatic person, believing honesty and truth should always prevail, rather than the social dances so many people play daily in their lives. If someone asks me how I'm doing, I tell them the truth. If I'm having a bad day, I tell them so. Of course that's not what they wanted to hear at all, but I was being honest, as usual.

Hummer medicine has taught me to assess the situation and other person before I answer. If the person is a stranger and doesn't look or feel as though he cares personally about me, I give them the stock "I'm fine" answer. I've noticed one thing about hummers – they never waste their time on something that doesn't produce fruition. I've learned over the years not to waste my time with people or situations that don't have objectives or goals similar to mine.

I've learned a little bit of diplomacy (even though I'm sure it will take lifetimes for me), a great deal more patience and attention to focusing always on my goal from the Hummingbird People. What great teachers they continue to be for me—and for you, if you will let them.

Oh, yes, I found out about the "nectar" that Sam was grilling me about, too. It's the nectar of life, if you will, the sweet, moment-to-moment joys that are always there for us if we will just notice them. Sometimes in our busy, stressed-out lives, we fail to see anything at all except what is right in front of us, staring us down or demanding our attention. Hummer medicine brings the little daily joys of life back into perspective, back into your life in a wonderful, quiet, gentle way.

A long time ago I would never have "wasted" my morning by sitting on a bench in a rose garden. A decade later I can sit and enjoy the small nuances that the flow of the River of Life directs past me, note them, thank them and be a part of them.

If I hadn't been sitting on that bench in the rose garden, cup of coffee in hand, I'd never have seen that hummer take a bath in that rose. For me, it was a symbolic blessing that now I too know how to "take a bath in a rose," in my own way—by sitting quietly, praying, thinking and feeling, and allowing the beauty of the day and of our Mother Earth to harmonize within myself.

Thunderbeings

hen I was seven years old and my two younger siblings were six and three, respectively, a horrendous thunderstorm came up early one morning, around 4 a.m. It was still dark out, and the wind was howling like a woman screaming. I was scared to death, awakened out of a deep sleep in my own room. Frightened, I ran to my parents' room, wanting to get into bed with them to be safe from this giant storm outside our house.

Of course, they sent me back to my bed, but by this time my sister and brother, Nancy and Gary, had been awakened too by the crash of thunder and the slashing of rain against the house. It sounded like a major hail storm. We all crowded into Gary's bed, an Army cot, like a bunch of baby rabbits huddled together for warmth – only it wasn't for warmth, it was for protection against that storm. We had no sooner snuggled together under the quilt and blanket, grabbing onto one another, when a bolt of lightning struck the metal clothesline just outside the bedroom window.

The entire room blew up with light so blinding that it was

incredible. The horrendous sound of thunder crashed down upon us, making all of us shriek in unadulterated terror. Worse, just moments before the lightning hit, the hair on our bodies had stood on end. We knew we were in for it, but had no concept of just *how* we were in for it.

The lightning hit a pie tin that my mother had set by the clothes-line for feeding the cats each morning. We heard the pie tin being struck, heard the metallic sound as it soared upward and then banged back down on the ground several times after the strike. We were crying and so scared. We didn't even want to get out of the bed for fear another bolt would get us before we got to our parents' bed-room!

As the storm continued to howl around the house, and I huddled in the warmth and darkness with my two shaking siblings, I vividly recalled the terror I had felt because of thunder when I was five years old. I recalled being so terrified that I'd run screaming hysterically to wherever my mother was. One time, she laughed, picked me up and told me not to be afraid of the sound in the sky. All it was, she said, pointing to the roiling, dark, pregnant clouds above us, were giants kicking a tin can around between them. Each time a giant kicked the tin can, we'd hear it down on Earth as a rumble of thunder.

I have never felt so relieved, and I remember that the fear went away after I had grasped the concept that there was an invisible giant or two up in those storm clouds. My mother returned me to the ground and I remember feeling relieved and that these giants weren't going to hurt me after all; they were merely playing "kick the can" just like us kids played it with one another!

That memory surfaced as I quaked and shook beneath the covers with Gary and Nancy, but this storm was too close for comfort, too frightening and overpowering. The sound was brutal on my sensitive "dog ears."

After that particular storm I began to try to understand these giants better, probably realizing that if I understood, then I would stop being afraid. Between the ages of seven and nine, I would spend hours on my back in a field, studying the fluffy cumulus clouds that drifted lazily across the sky. My mother had told me that I could use my mind's energy to move the clouds, and I practiced this until it became an art form.

As I began to work with the Cloud People, as we called them, I was made to understand that they were smaller, less powerful spirits who worked for Father Sky, who was the big boss. However, my father told me about Thunderbeings, huge giants who were invisible but very powerful spirits whose job it was to gather the clouds and create the violence so that a thunderstorm would arise. Father Sky was the chief, but the Thunderbeings were his lieutenants and the rest of the clouds were privates.

My father would tell me about these fantastically powerful beings who are invisible to the naked eye, whose sole job it was to create the storms that raged around Mother Earth. He told me that I could see them with my third eye, but as hard as I tried, I couldn't see a thing. However, my fear of thunderstorms had transformed into one of absolute awe and excitement each time one swept across the dry, desertlike region of Ontario, Oregon, where we lived at the time.

I recall one thunderstorm in particular that occurred when I was nine years old. I saw the fluffy white cumulus clouds building into thick, high towers in the distance and heard the far-off thunder, knowing that it was coming our way. Out back, near our cow barn, was a huge pile of dried manure. This manure pile stretched about 40 feet and was about 15 feet high. Because it was dry, we kids would play on and around it constantly. It was the only "mountain" on the flat Ontario terrain.

This thunderstorm brewing west of us was enormous. It was far larger than any storm I'd ever seen roll across the dry Oregon desert. An excitement filled me, one of eager anticipation. I didn't know why. I was always happy to have a thunderstorm roll over now, realizing that those invisible giants, the Thunderbeings, were amassing, moving and creating storms that would give Mother Earth a drink of necessary water for her and all her relations.

The wind spirits began to whip around me, dancing, tugging at my clothes and at my long brown hair. A thrill shot through me as I intuitively raced up to the top of our manure mountain. The storm was immense, brooding dark gray on the bottom with cauliflower, bubbling cumulus formations shooting skyward to at least 50,000 feet in altitude. The wind grew stronger, no longer playful, but sharp gusts warning me of the approaching storm.

Out of some instinct, as the lightning danced closer and closer to me, the storm now moving directly over our home, I threw my small, skinny arms skyward, my hands outstretched, open. And I laughed for the sheer joy of feeling the actual invisible power of this approaching Thunderbeing.

Then a strange thing happened. I felt wild tingling begin in the tips of all my fingers, and quickly, like a bolt of lightning, it raced up my arms, into my head and down through my body. I felt electrical, as if I had stuck my finger into an electric outlet. It was a heady, thrilling moment. The wind roared and gusted around me. I inhaled the sweet, fresh scent of approaching rain deep into my lungs. My hair whipped around me like live snakes. My body was buffeted by invisible hands so powerful that it almost made me lose my balance. The sensations going through me were incredible, and I stood there as the electrical activity raced among me, that storm and the Earth.

As I stood there, an old memory, a déjà vu, stirred deep in my unconscious. It was a past-life memory of being a young priestess in another country, stretching her arms skyward, the lightning dancing around her, yet never touching her or harming her. The memory itself was like a lightning bolt – gone as quickly as it had come.

I don't know how long I stood there, probably until the rains came. And then I ran down off the pile of manure to the safety of the house because I hated getting wet!

I had never realized what had taken place that day until much later in my life when Sam, my teacher, sat listening to my story about that incident. He kind of smiled, settled his cowboy hat, a beat-up old straw hat that had too many smudges of dirt along the brim, and looked directly at me.

"You know, they're called Thunderbeings."

Eagerly, I leaned forward. We were sitting out in the hills of California near a sage patch where we'd just gathered some sage ceremonially, and we were taking a break from the hot Sun overhead.

"What can you tell me about them?" I prayed he'd open up and tell me something, because rarely would he divulge much of anything.

Taking a piece of the recently picked, velvet, white and green sage, he stuck a leaf in his mouth and leaned back against a large black lava rock. "Among the Cherokee, if you have Thunderbeing medicine . . ." Then he just shook his head, his smile widening.

Frustrated, I said, "Sam! What about this medicine?"

"You have it."

"What?"

"The Thunderbeings have chosen you to carry their medicine." He waved his hand vaguely upward toward the white clouds that

dotted the pale blue sky. "Usually, if someone tries for this medicine, he/she gets hit by lightning. A lot of people are killed this way.
Most don't survive, or if they do, they aren't the same."

"I wasn't hit by lightning."

"No, but you don't always have to be struck. What you were feeling when you were nine was the actual energy that is transferred
between the Thunderbeings and Mother Earth. Not many people
ever get to experience that. You did. It means you're in tune with
them."

I wrapped my arms around my drawn-up knees. "Tell me more."

"The guys I know in Oklahoma who have this medicine . . .
well, they can call a Thunderbeing. And when they do, it knocks
them unconscious — maybe for an hour, maybe for a day at a time."

"What happens when they wake up?"

"They have a message or a vision of some kind."

Fascinated, I said, "I've never had that happen."

He chewed thoughtfully on a second sage leaf. "Maybe you don't
have to," he murmured.

"But," I searched, looking up at the sky and clouds, "what does
Thunderbeing medicine do?"

"What do storms do?"

I groaned, knowing full well Sam was going to play his endless cir-
cular game of words with me. By then I was used to it, but that
didn't mean I liked it any more than before, because I didn't. "They
nourish Mother Earth. They give water back to her so that all things
can continue to live."

"That's a pretty tall order, isn't it?" he said, his eyes narrowing
speculatively.

I moved uncomfortably, knowing Sam wanted me to realize the
observation I'd made and apply it to myself. "Okay," I began halt-
ingly, "maybe, in some small way, I give back to my relatives?"

"Good. Go on."

"On to what?" I got up, growling, dusting off the seat of my Levi's
and giving him a dirty look in the interim.

"What else?"

There were days when I could take his good-natured prodding but
today wasn't one of them. "Dammit, Sam, just tell me okay?"

He gave me a very patient look and a smile.

I felt like hell. I felt embarrassed because I'd lost my temper and
he'd never lost his with me. But then, he was twenty years my senior

and more mature, I told myself grumpily. Throwing up my arms, I walked around the area beneath the shade of the pin oak where he sat.

"You were in the Navy," Sam began quietly. "You were a weather forecaster for three years. You can't tell me that you don't know something about clouds, how they're made and what they do."

His reminder stung me even more and I glared at him. I sat down opposite him on a smooth reddish-colored rock. "Do you want a lot of scientific gobbledygook?" I demanded tightly.

"No. Just look at it all symbolically."

I tried to soothe my shame and embarrassment. Sam didn't deserve my short temper or lack of patience, but then I'd had trouble with both all my life. What was new? Grimly, I forced myself to take an overview of weather forecasting, of my understanding on a scientific level about clouds and their formation, their intrinsic tie to Mother Earth.

"They," I said waspishly, "transform. The water on the Earth and in the rivers, streams and oceans, is lifted invisibly to the sky and the condensation that occurs because of hot and cold factors create the clouds."

"Very good." He smiled a little and stretched out so his shoulders and head were against the rock, as though it were a pillow, and he pushed the cowboy hat forward so that it covered nearly all his face. "What's the key word in all those things you said?"

My mouth twisted at one corner and I tried to patiently sort through my definition. "Transformation, I guess . . ."

"Right. So how does that apply to you? To what you do or will do in the future?"

"Transform things?" I guessed, not very sure at all of what Sam was getting at.

"Bingo."

I should have felt relief because I had a "right" answer, but I didn't. I sat there a good fifteen minutes chewing on that one. In the meantime, Sam dozed off, his soft snore punctuating the lazy, hot California afternoon. Unhappy, I got up and stalked off to the hillside of sage. We still needed more for ceremony, and I dearly loved talking with the plants and gathering the wonderful, aromatic herb.

As I asked permission to pick a few stalks from each plant, I was mulling over Sam's needling me into realizing that Thunderbeing medicine was actually about transformation. As I picked, my temper cooled and my feelings of shame and embarrassment dissolved. I tried to look at my life from the perspective of transformation.

By the time I was eighteen years old, we'd moved twenty-two times, not just in one state, either, but all over the West. Going into the Navy when I was eighteen required a different kind of transformation – one of leaving home and going into a very rigid military atmosphere, something few women had ever done. And that had certainly been a transforming experience if there had ever been one! I had learned lessons about myself, about relationships, about men and about so many other things.

The more I picked sage on the hillside, the more deeply I went into looking at my life as one of ongoing transformation. I had left the Navy and taken up professional astrology. (My mother had studied astrology and had allowed me to read her books when I was nine years old, so I got my love of this science way back then.)

As an astrological counselor, I saw that I made a difference in about 50% of my clients' lives, but I also saw a more pressing need in the field of health and astrology. I taught myself medical astrology and worked for a decade on a scientific footing to prove what I knew and to discover a way of looking at the chart medically. I discovered the Med-Scan Technique, and it's 95% accurate, even to this day.

Because I'd gone into the health field from a metaphysical perspective, homeopathy, a complementary form of medicine practiced all over the world (although only minimally in the U.S.), became my next transformation. In homeopathy I discovered a form of medicine that truly transforms in the most positive of ways and is the only system of medicine on the face of the Earth that cures. So I then became a homeopathic consultant, transforming people's lives in that way.

By the time I had finished collecting another bag of sage and had gone to rest under the pin oak, Sam had awakened from his nap. He was sitting there with a canteen in his hands, sipping the warm water. I sat down and gave him an apologetic look. "I see what you mean about transformation, about how it applies to me, to my life and to the work I do."

He grunted and sat up, crossing his legs, his dusty cowboy boots scarred with age and wear. Capping the canteen, he offered it to me. "You're like a lightning bolt in some ways," he said. "You're a catalyst in the lives of other people. That's an aspect of Thunderbeing medicine. You don't get knocked out, but the people, your clients, are rattled or shaken by your insights into them. You know that a ceremony, a song, a homeopathic remedy, a correct herb, can all change a person's life for the better."

I took the canteen and swallowed a long gulp of the water. I appreciated Sam's insights. I capped the canteen and set it aside. "So I shock others into an awareness about themselves on some level?"

He smiled. "You got it."

"If I'm so good at this, why can't I catalyze myself?" I grumbled.

With a hearty laugh, Sam slowly unwound and stood up. "That's my job."

Ever since those two years of training with Sam, wherever I go, the Thunderbeings come with me. In November of 1990, I was invited down to São Paulo, Brazil, to present a workshop to scientists and medical doctors about medical astrology. For the week that I was in São Paulo, there was a thunderstorm every day. My host, Miguel Ferrari, told me that it was highly unusual for there to be storms in the city at that time of year. Further, the storms were so large and devastating that they literally flooded parts of this city of fourteen million people.

When I left with Miguel and his family to spend a week in the Amazon jungle, we first stopped off at Cortina, in Minas Gerais, the mining state of Brazil. We toured tourmaline mines and quartz crystal mines and saw some of the most beautiful gems I'd ever seen. I had sung songs for the spirits of this incredibly beautiful land while there. I had made a small medicine wheel for them. When it was time to leave and fly on to Manaus, which is set at the headwaters of the Amazon, the most amazing and spectacular thunderstorm arose. It was a storm of such devastation that it knocked two hundred-year-old trees down across the two-lane highway, blocking us from going anywhere.

As I sat in the van while my husband and Miguel worked with twenty other people who had left their cars to try to remove the huge tree from the road that dusk, a Thunderbeing called my name. I turned to the window and looked out, hearing his deep voice vibrating telepathically in my mind. He told me that the mountain spirit of the area didn't want me to leave but rather to stay a few more days and perform more healing ceremonies for the spirits of the region. The mountain spirit had asked the Thunderbeing to create a storm of such magnitude that it would stop me from leaving! I was thunderstruck, to say the least, having not even thought of my presence in the area in that way. I didn't even have my personal pipe with me. I only had my songs, my heart and my need to give back to all my relations.

I begged the Thunderbeing to relent, to let us pass, to stop the rain. Within fifteen minutes, the storm abated and within half an hour, right at twilight, the sky was miraculously clear of clouds and storm. It was magical. I felt humbled by the request of the powerful mountain spirit near Governador Valadares, the gateway to the land of gems and minerals. But I couldn't stay. I mentally sent a promise to that huge mountain that if I ever returned to Brazil, I would bring my pipe, stand at his base and perform a healing ceremony for him and his relations.

No matter where I go in the world, a thunderstorm will crop up about twelve hours before I arrive, during the time I'm there or roughly twelve hours after I've left the area. I'm reminded of a time I flew into Los Angeles where I was to stay at a woman's house and give a two-day workshop on medical astrology. She was a very controlling individual, what we term a "powerstalker," but at the time, I didn't realize it. However, fifteen minutes after my arrival, a thunderstorm took place and lightning struck the transmitter on the power pole right next to her apartment! Needless to say, I paid attention, and I knew that in this particular case, it was a warning. By being on guard, I averted a lot of unnecessary problems for myself as well as for the people who took this workshop. The Thunderbeings were warning me, and for once, I paid attention.

Do you have Thunderbeing medicine? If you have an intrinsic love for and awe of thunderstorms, you probably do. If you've been struck by lightning, then the medicine is already yours. This isn't a medicine to play around with lightly. If you take up the medicine, it means that your life will forever be one of continual transformation on personal levels. But it also means that you'll have the responsibility of knowing that when you meet a person or are involved in a situation, you will be a natural catalyst.

We need catalysts in our world to jog us out of our ruts, our blinders-on way of leading our lives.

Sam was certainly a catalyst in my life and, needless to say, he had Thunderbeing medicine. My life changed irrevocably after two years with him. Since understanding this medicine better, I see catalysts all around me. Some are waging a war for Mother Earth, and they are our environmentalists on the front lines. Some are waging war in the name of the homeless, to help them. Some catalyze on a smaller but nonetheless important scale.

We each have a role to play, a path we've chosen to walk in this lifetime. If yours is the life of a catalyst, large or small, then I especially honor your course, because it's not an easy mantle to wear or to keep wearing. It brings many responsibilities and demands, but from my perspective, I can't think of anything more healing than helping to effect positive changes for "all our relations." Can you?

Vortexes of Mother Earth

There are sacred spots all over Mother Earth; in fact, all of her is sacred. Just like our bodies and the energies surrounding them, Mother Earth has an aura, too.

The first layer of aura that surrounds our physical body is called the *etheric body*. This layer looks like cross-hatching or like a tightly woven web all around our form.

The etheric body is like a template or blueprint of the physical form; it holds all the information about how to make the physical body during this lifetime. Lodged within the etheric body, on the front and back, are seven major chakras, or power stations, that convert prana, the energy surrounding us, into energy that our bodies can eventually use. The Far Eastern religions all know about these energy-converting centers. In fact the acupuncture system recognizes not only the major chakra centers but also the secondary ones. Our etheric bodies are like electric grids filled with power stations that are constantly sucking in prana. The chakras have propellerlike blades, or petals, that whirl and turn either clockwise or counterclockwise. The movement of these blades stirs up the River of Life (the cosmic soup, if you will), and the submolecular particles are drawn into the chakras where translation and change take place.

Energy can be changed but it can never be destroyed, and the duty of the chakras is to create a transformative process that can feed not only the physical body through the endocrine glands and the nerves but also the rest of the layers of the aura. The whirling motion creates a vortex of energy. The smaller chakras are located on the palms of the hands, the soles of the feet, the knees, the shoulders and so forth, and they whirl and turn, too. So the human body is literally a walking vortex of sorts.

Mother Earth, similarly, has an etheric body around her that acts as a layer of protection. However, at her North and South Poles, there are now holes in her etheric body that have been caused by humans. We too can get holes or tears in the etheric body, which then leaks and bleeds us of the vital life-force energy by which good health is maintained and harmony is kept in place. People who are alcoholics or drug-users often have an etheric body that literally looks like someone has taken a shotgun to it; the etheric body looks like a sieve.

Mother Earth has a major chakra system as well as a secondary system, just as we do. Each one is a whirling vortex spinning either clockwise or counterclockwise. She has an energy grid system that dowsers and other sensitive people can feel. Sometimes people can locate such an area by using a pendulum.

Ancient cultures, because the people were right-brained (that is to say, they were in touch with their intuition and their psychic/clairvoyant abilities and were believers in many aspects of metaphysics), often built their sacred temples on these Earth chakras in order to take advantage of the spiraling energy that reached skyward toward the cosmos or toward their goddesses and gods.

As times changed and one civilization fell to another, new temples or structures were built on these sites. Those who knew and understood the energies utilized them. Those who didn't would always come away from these sites feeling better somehow, inexplicably uplifted or perhaps healed on some level.

Christianity might pooh-pooh metaphysics, but the founders built their mighty religious centers right on the same sites that other ancient civilizations had used for their temples! At the highest levels, especially in the Catholic Church, the leaders knew about these sites — what they were and how they operated. That is why so many of the beautiful European abbeys and churches, such as Chartres in France, feel so powerful. People feel moved when they enter these structures, but what they're really feeling is the power and energy of the chakra, moving and transforming the cosmic energy into another form that Mother Earth can digest and utilize. This is not to say that the power of people's prayers aren't present in those churches, because they are; they have a power of their own. But it can't match the power of one of these vortexes.

The Druids had, perhaps, the most far-reaching and profound effects in working with Mother Earth's chakras. The priestesses and priests maintained the Mother Goddess worship, which included the caretaking of Mother Earth, for thousands of years. They were a living bridge between the old goddess religions and Christianity, carrying it forward despite the rise of patriarchy and the worship of male deities.

The Druids did something very special all over Europe, North America and South America: they not only searched out and found many of the chakras of Mother Earth, they also created weblike lines of energy that would flow between these points across the globe to move energy and to keep our Mother in harmony and balance.

Druids sailed across the Atlantic. They met and taught the wise women and men of Turtle Island (North America). There they worked with the mound-builders in the Mississippi Valley to create a series of temple mounds that were located on Earth chakras in order to keep those vortexes healthy and sound. These mounds extend from the Great Lakes all the way down toward Mexico. One of the greatest and most important of these mounds, called the Great Serpent Mound, is found in southern Ohio. If you ever have a question about what a vortex is, go visit this one. I guarantee it will change your life, blast open your closed chakras and set you right with yourself. Those in the know always go to this mound for the solstice and equinox ceremonies — and they are Native Americans, Wiccans and holy people from South America.

The mounds are a line of transmitter stations, which keep a very important north-south energy running at all times. If you draw a line down through Mexico and into South America, you will find that major Mayan, Aztec and Incan pyramids were placed over these vortex points, too. Further, the Nazca Plain of Peru was and is a major beacon point/vortex for outer-space traffic to hone in on in order to find Mother Earth.

The powerful grid running north-south in this region isn't the only one. The Druids worked with peoples of all tribes and nations around the world, creating stone circles to denote places of power or vortex energy. That is not to say that peoples of other nations, particularly those who were close to the Mother anyway, didn't already know about these sites. They did. They erected their own kinds of ceremonial altars or stone circles to indicate sacred sites.

There are other places on Mother Earth that are extremely powerful but have no indicator such as a church, a stone circle or anything else to bring our attention to them. The Native Americans would often disguise a site by not putting any indicator on the area. They knew most Anglos would never feel the energy, so they would not violate the site.

MOTHER EARTH BREATHES

Mother Earth breathes, just as we do. Among Native Americans and Tibetan cultures, the process is known as her lunar (night) and solar (day) breaths. There are areas where she actually exhales or inhales. In the Southwest area, the Hopi region known as Black Mesa is where she expels her lunar breath each night. The resulting wind from the exhalation is known as *spirit wind*. Anyone who has experienced this incredible phenomenon will know immediately what it is, because it has a sound that is highly unusual, almost eerie, although not in a negative sense. I've seen tree limbs crack in the wake of the spirit wind as it shrieks through our canyon on some nights. It comes suddenly, without warning, and has nothing to do with the prevailing weather or its patterns.

Tibet is known as the region where the Mother inhales her solar breath. Anyone who has been in a cave, especially a large, deep one, has experienced an incredible sense of nurturing energy, as though in the Mother's womb, as well as the breathing of the cave. These regions where she breathes are also powerful points on her surface. The Hopi zealously guard the Black Mesa area for many reasons both secret and sacred. They are the keepers of this mesa, and they are charged with its well-being just as the Druids were charged to keep their vortexes clean, operational and in good repair.

Just as our bodies' chakras can open, close or get blown out by a severe shock or trauma, so can those of Mother Earth. Ideally, when we are in perfect harmony, all our chakras are open and running. However, most of us aren't there yet, so our chakras are at different stages of opening or closing down or are clogged with positive ions which I call "goo." Some or all of their petals/propellers might have been damaged, shredded or torn off by some terrible trauma or shock.

Mother Earth is in a situation similar to ours. All her chakra points are not open but might be shut down, clogged with etheric debris or ripped so that the energy isn't being funneled out or in properly. The Druids of long ago used song, sounds and ceremonies to keep a chakra open, cleaned and in proper working order. That is what the series of mounds throughout the Mississippi Valley were about: taking care of major chakra points in order to ensure the smooth, operational running of the north-south energy grid through that region.

EFFECTS OF CLOGGING MOTHER EARTH'S CHAKRAS

When these chakras get clogged with debris, they slow or simply shut down and refuse to work. That means that the energy flowing into that region is diminished or denied. When this happens it will, over time, deprive a region of fundamental, life-giving energy. The results can be catastrophic. The latest example of this is California. No one has ever seen such a series of devastating natural disasters. First, a series of earthquakes, then fires, now mudslides.

This past September [1993], I went back to my original "home" where my first vision was given to me: the sequoias of California, high on the western slopes of the Sierra Mountains. I had been going back there, usually at the autumnal equinox, for almost sixteen years. The sequoias were a real power center (I've written about them and my experiences with them in other chapters), but it had been ten years since I'd last visited my friends. When I reached them this time, the sacred energy that used to be there was gone. I was in shock as I walked through the groves of my friends. I asked them, "What happened?" They told me, sadly, that they could no longer hold back the negative energy of Los Angeles with all its gang wars, the city having become a war zone. Their energy had been moved.

My trees told me that because they could no longer pump the vital, life-giving energy into Mother Earth in this region of southern California and part of Arizona (the Grand Canyon), it was now barren. Without positive energy being given to the region, the negative or dark forces could run amok without any interference and could literally take over.

It was September of 1993 when I was told this. Shortly after that, devastation hit southern California. Earthquakes have been proliferating throughout this region, including the Grand Canyon, indicating that the land is showing the stress of the loss of this vital, life-giving, balancing energy.

It isn't going to stop for southern California, because a major energy center has shut down. Some day, I'm sure, this vortex will reopen, but right now, it has stopped completely. The pollution by humanity both by car engines and by prejudice, hatred and anger has done even more damage to the sacred energies of this region. Because the energy has moved, it leaves the region wide open for all kinds of natural disasters. These "disasters" are Mother Earth's way of cleansing the region, getting rid of the disease that has resulted in her going out of harmony, thereby causing the energy that rightfully belongs there for her continued health to leave. She will do everything in her power to cleanse the area — and I've got to say that fire, rains and mudslides are certainly cleansing activities. So is wind and so are earthquakes.

I don't pretend to be a prognosticator of future events in an area, but I can speak from my knowledge of the gridwork and etheric body of Mother Earth. Once they are messed with, then disasters to cleanse a region are not at all uncommon. The "infection" in southern California has created disharmony for her, and I know she won't stand still for it. If you had a wound on your body, you'd instantly cleanse it to get rid of infection, wouldn't you? So will she.

When an area is sufficiently cleansed, then the energy will return and the chakra will gradually, over time, open up and begin to spin again, absorbing and transferring the life-giving energy back into the region. We can do our part to help keep a power point clean and functioning or to stop the encroachment of negative energy.

REPLENIƧHING CHAKRA CENTERƧ

Many times when I go into a chakra region in Sedona, Arizona, I carry my flute or drum or take the pipe or a ceremony into the vortex to give back to it. I take nothing from a vortex because that's not my job as a pipe carrier. Each song that is sung, each drum that is beaten, each pipe that is smoked, each rattle that is shaken will bring positive energy into the vortex if you're coming from the heart. You don't need to know about ceremony or be a pipe carrier in order to bring light, love or positive energy into a chakra. I meet a number of other like-minded, sensitive people on the trail, either going in or coming out, who are also carrying ceremonial items such as the above, to do the same thing as I have done — help support the region in a positive way.

A friend of mine, Michele Burdet of Switzerland, is a dowser and during a recent visit, we traded information about her findings in the great churches of Europe by using her techniques and knowledge. I invited her to use her dowsing abilities on the land we caretake, especially where my hogan is built over a vortex. By using her own techniques, she told me it was feminine energy, a sacred and ceremonial energy center. She was right.

You can feel the gridwork and chakras without even realizing it. In training my facilitators, I put them through several exercises that help to bring out and emphasize their own natural abilities to sense these sacred areas. First, go to an area that you like. Often this is a high-energy area of some kind. Sit down. Close your eyes and get comfortable, perhaps in a meditative state. Take a deep breath through your nose, deep into your body, and then release it through your mouth. Do this three times. This is an Apache breathing technique that is designed to switch you from the left hemisphere of your brain, which will keep you anchored in the third dimension, over to the right hemisphere, where you can connect directly into the cosmos and into your own intuitive self in order to feel these vibrations.

Once this is done, just relax and feel, see or sense what comes to you in the form of impressions. When in the region of an Earth chakra there is always a spinning sensation that comes from your root chakra at the base of your tailbone, and you will rock. You will rock, usually, in an east-west direction or in a north-south direction. These are indicators that you're on a pretty powerful spot.

I never enter an area such as this without first giving an offering of cornmeal, tobacco or food to the spirits who inhabit the region. Then I always ask permission; I ask if I may walk into that area. I explain that I come in a sacred way to give back to the place, not to take from it. If I am going to sing, I tell them I am going to sing. I wait for either a yes or a no. You'll feel it, believe me. If I get permission, I go into the area.

There are some sacred areas that are only female or only male, and the area wants only one gender or the other. I know of a number of places up in Oak Creek Canyon [Sedona] that are strictly male areas, and many medicine men take their male students there. I would never think of going into those areas because I am a woman and of different energy. To do so is to be disrespectful and is also to influence the male energy that is there for a good reason. Honor these differences.

This is only scratching the surface regarding the chakra centers, the vortexes, that cover Mother Earth's etheric body. You can help her to get better, even to get well, if you work with these special areas of energy by coming from the heart and giving something of yourself, such as a song, an offering, the playing of a musical instrument or whatever else you might think of that would be appropriate.

Our Mother is hurting; she is diseased, thanks to us humans. What we've done wrong, we can right. So go seek out these places and give back. I know she'll appreciate your generosity of heart and spirit.

Temple Mounds

*I*n my previous chapter about vortexes, I outlined their metaphysical blueprint and discussed how and why they work. Now,
I'd like to share some instances of working with vortex energy. I
hope you find something useful in my experiences.

As I mentioned before, the Great Serpent Mound of southern
Ohio is a fairly large vortex of immense power and usefulness to
Mother Earth's continuing health. Because I lived in northeast
Ohio for fourteen years, I was very familiar with the mounds that
are found in that lovely state, north to south.

A good friend of mine, Tom McKibbins, had a special interest in
mounds because he was an amateur archaeologist and had a vari-
ety of Native American genes, including Cree, Cherokee and Lenni
Lenape, Sacajawea's people. (Sometime I'll tell you about a very
powerful and ancient medicine piece he found, and the incredible
things that happened to him after the find.)

Tom used to take me out on weekends and teach me about the
mounds. In Ohio there are a lot of beech, oak, maple, elm and

many other hardwood trees. He told me that the Druids had crossed the Atlantic thousands of years ago and had met, mingled with and lived among the Native Americans.

Each nation brought its own particular wisdom, knowledge and experience to the table and it was shared. During the mound period, the Indians worked closely with their Druid friends in establishing powerful energy connections from the Great Lakes all the way down through Mexico to South America. They did this by building mounds according to ceremony at the correct time of year to ensure that the location of the the mound was perfectly aligned with a certain star so that it would collect all the cosmic energies. The power of this particular Ohio grid line was enhanced by the building of mounds and pyramids (Incan, Mayan and Aztec) all along it. At each chakra site, the vortex energy moves clockwise or counterclockwise; the structures were built to reflect this movement and to intensify it. They kept the vortexes clean and sacred through ceremony, song and the purity of intent of those who cared for these sites.

Tom told me that some mounds were burial sites; many were not. Some were vortex power stations, "on-line," if you will, just like telephone poles. The mounds were electric substations, gathering the energy along the grid line, enhancing and empowering it, and then sending it onward to the next sacred mound.

There was also another kind of mound, the temple mound. This was the highest, most powerful class of mounds. Tom taught me how to visually discern the difference, although a sensitive person could feel the difference. The Druids chose certain vortexes as temple sites for sacred, seasonal ceremonies. They would always plant two beech trees as "gate guardians." Beech trees, for the Druids, were always symbolic of female energy. If the vortexes at the temple site had masculine energy, then two oak trees were planted as gate guardians. If the energy of the vortex site was androgynous (comprised of both female and male energy), then one beech and one oak were planted as gate guardians.

Tom's teachings were awesome and I appreciated his showing me what he had learned over the years as an archaeologist and as a Native American. He showed me how to look for the gate guardians, for to enter a vortex, burial mound or temple mound site without permission could be a serious breach of metaphysical ethics.

The gate guardians are living spirits, and the beech and oak are very long-lived trees. They can survive for three or four hundred years, sometimes more. These spirits hold a living, ongoing trust, which is not linear, to guard the vortex/mound, no matter what type it is. Once I had located the actual gate I gave a gift of food, tobacco or cornmeal to each guardian. As I gave the gift, I told the tree my name and my reason for being there and I asked permission to proceed to the mound.

Before going in, I knew whether it was a burial mound, a vortex substation or a temple. I normally didn't go to burial mounds because I regard them as sacred and feel it is better to leave them alone. The spirits that remain at these mounds don't want human intervention. On occasion, I had been guided to go to some of them to release a particular spirit but that was by request, not according to some decision I had made for that spirit beforehand.

Some of these temple mounds were nothing to mess around with. I found that out by accident understanding that there is no such thing as an accident, and that it was a synchronistic event. One day, after giving my gifts and getting the go-ahead, I stepped through the invisible gate between the guardians. The instant I was through the gate, vertigo struck me so hard and swiftly that I fell to my knees. I was shocked by the jellylike weakness in my knees as I fell forward on my hands. I shook my head, dizzy and completely disoriented.

I had never encountered such a powerful, whirling vortex before, nor have I since that incident. I was on my hands and knees for a good five minutes, desperately trying to reorient myself. I looked up and everything seemed different. The trees within the invisible circle of the temple mound were different. What was it? I slowly got to my feet, took a few tottering steps forward and anchored myself. I felt strange. The dizziness had abated to a degree, but I could still feel it tugging and pulling at me.

Turning back, I saw the gate guardians. Relieved that I wasn't lost, I turned back. I didn't see a mound anywhere, yet I knew there had to be one because the beech and oak trees stood tall and stately, indicating one was near. The brush was so thick and so high, and the trees were so close together that I could barely see ten feet in any direction.

I closed my eyes, trying to center myself, but it was impossible. Which way to go? Normally, I instinctively knew in which direction a mound was located. Not this time! I walked a few steps and turned around. The gate guardians were gone. I whirled around and around in a panic, trying to find them. I felt out of focus and dizzy.

At the time I didn't realize it, but this vortex's power was interdimensional. That meant that as soon as I had stepped through the invisible gate, the door into the other dimensions had opened and I had literally, in a physical form, walked into another dimension.

My fear was well-founded, because as I stumbled through the brush, completely disoriented, my own internal radar was of no use to guide me. I knew I was in trouble. For the first time in my life, I understood on a very deep, gut level what it feels like to be lost in the woods. I had been raised in the mountains where my father had taught me to track, to know my directions, day or night, and I'd never gotten lost. I had trekked the Cascades of Oregon and California without fear, but there in the woodlands of Ohio, I was good and lost.

I sat down. I had to try to center myself. I had to put my fear aside and concentrate. The feeling I had was that if I couldn't settle down and reestablish my harmony, I'd never get out of those woods alive. It was a foolish feeling, but that was where I was at. I closed my eyes and tried to meditate. It did no good. I couldn't center; I was out of balance.

Disheartened, I slowly got to my feet and looked around. Everything seemed distorted. Trees seemed to be leaning but not grotesquely, just differently. This was my first experience with altered realities while consciously awake and not in a dream state. While it was going down, I couldn't put two and two together.

I stumbled around for the next half-hour and somehow circled back to the spot where I had meditated. I hadn't moved in a circle and I knew it. Yet there I was, right back where I had started. I looked around, my gaze trying to probe the late-afternoon woodlands for the gate guardians. They were nowhere to be seen. Panic was still driving me, and I had a terrible feeling that if I didn't get out of there by nightfall, I'd be in deep trouble.

Stilling my panic, I tried to think. The only thought that congealed through my dizziness and apprehension was to ask for help. It was so simple, and I, more than most, knew better. It was the first thing I should have done, not the last. Castigating myself, I staggered to a stop. Dizziness assailed me again. I grabbed the branch of a bush, closed my eyes and prayed for help. I asked for directions out of the temple mound area. At that point, I didn't even care about finding the mound. I just wanted to get out of that crazy, mixed-up energy field that distorted my own senses and state of balance.

I opened my eyes and a bird suddenly appeared no more than five feet in front of me, perched on a brush branch. It looked at me, gave a *cheep* and flew off to the north. My heart pounded with relief; I knew this was the sign I had prayed for. I knew the Great Spirit had sent her to me to become my guide and lead me out of this place.

The bird would fly about ten feet, stay just close enough for me to see her, wait until I got within a couple of feet and then fly off again. I followed the bird, stumbling, falling and staggering through the thick foliage. Suddenly I stopped, my eyes widening. There, right in front of me, were three mounds. They weren't huge. They were sheltered by the stately, sacred beech and oak trees all around and they stood in a line, east to west.

I stood there breathing hard, completely out of breath and still trying to adjust to the energy. I was stymied at first because I'd never before seen three mounds in one place. Usually there was just one. I made a note to ask Tom about it – providing I could get out in the first place and then find the location once again. I wasn't very sure that I could. Slowly, I circled the three mounds. They were small, about 50 to 100 feet in diameter. The first mound was the largest, the second one was next in size and the third was the smallest. I knew the energy grid ran north and south, yet this temple mound site was going east and west. Could that alignment explain the crazy energy that was throwing me completely out of kilter?

I felt my way around the temple mound and decided to sit on the smallest one, the third one. I gave gifts of food and cornmeal and then sat down. I felt like singing, so I did, my voice carrying as if I were in a wind tunnel. I stopped, stunned by the sound effects. What was going on? I tried singing again and the same thing happened. Shrugging, I closed my eyes and sang from my heart. As I sang, my voice felt stronger, deeper and more far-reaching than it ever had before. Normally, I can't sing more than two octaves, but there on that mound my voice had a wide range, from soprano to bass. Normally I was only an alto.

I don't know how long I sang, but the Sun was getting low on the horizon. I sat there and meditated for about half an hour. Nothing much happened, but then I wasn't expecting anything to happen – enough had already happened as far as I was concerned. I wasn't dizzy anymore and my aura had seemingly adjusted to the wild and crazy energy.

Before I left that magical place, I placed an eagle feather on one of the bushes on the first mound as a gift. I walked the entire circuit around the mounds leaving cornmeal and tobacco, thanking the mighty spirits of the temple for allowing me to come and participate with them.

By then my radar was back on, and I found it ridiculously easy to locate the gate guardians again. Amazed, I stepped beyond them. I stopped and felt different somehow. I turned, looking back into the temple area. I knew the mounds all had a circumference of energy around them that formed the actual circumference of the vortex. Puzzled, I stepped back through the invisible gate. I felt dizzy again, that powerful vertigo assailing me. I quickly stepped beyond the gate, back into "my" world.

Stymied, I made my way out of the woods and down a dirt road to the place where my car was parked. I pondered what I'd come upon, what I'd experienced. The answers didn't come right away. I told Tom about the mound and he didn't know what to make of it either. Over the next six months, I went back to the temple mound a number of times, and I took Tom with me. He found a number of pieces of evidence that it was a temple, but he left the evidence where it was. I honored him for that. Neither of us believed in desecrating a sacred site, ever. Over time, I came into contact with the spirits who were the other-dimensional caretakers of that highly active temple mound.

It was because of my experience with that strange set of mounds that I was led to the Great Serpent Mound in southern Ohio. I had been set up for one of the most powerful experiences I have ever had.

◆ B O O K   M A R K E T   O R D E R   F O R M ◆

BOOKS PUBLISHED BY LIGHT TECHNOLOGY PUBLISHING

		No. Copies	Total			No. Copies	Total			No. Copies	Total
Acupressure for the Soul	$11.95		$ ____	Shining the Light — Book IV	$14.95		$ ____	Soul Psychology	$14.95		$ ____
Arcturus Probe	$14.95		$ ____	**Robert Shapiro**				Beyond Ascension	$14.95		$ ____
Behold a Pale Horse	$25.00		$ ____	ETs and the Explorer Race	$14.95		$ ____	Hidden Mysteries	$14.95		$ ____
Cactus Eddie	$11.95		$ ____	The Explorer Race	$25.00		$ ____	Ascended Masters	$14.95		$ ____
Channelling: Evolutionary ...	$ 9.95		$ ____	**Arthur Fanning**				**Vywamus/Janet McClure**			
Color Medicine	$11.95		$ ____	Soul, Evolution, Father	$12.95		$ ____	AHA! The Realization Book	$11.95		$ ____
Forever Young	$ 9.95		$ ____	Simon	$ 9.95		$ ____	Light Techniques	$11.95		$ ____
Guardians of The Flame	$14.95		$ ____	**Wesley H. Bateman**				Sanat Kumara	$11.95		$ ____
Great Kachina	$11.95		$ ____	Dragons & Chariots	$ 9.95		$ ____	Scopes of Dimensions	$11.95		$ ____
Keys to the Kingdom	$14.95		$ ____	Knowledge From the Stars	$11.95		$ ____	The Source Adventure	$11.95		$ ____
Legend of the Eagle Clan	$12.95		$ ____	**Lynn Buess**				Prelude to Ascension	$29.95		$ ____
Living Rainbows	$14.95		$ ____	Children of Light, Children ...	$ 8.95		$ ____	**Leia Stinnett**			
Mahatma I & II	$19.95		$ ____	Numerology: Nuances ...	$12.65		$ ____	A Circle of Angels	$18.95		$ ____
Millennium Tablets	$14.95		$ ____	Numerology for the New Age	$11.00		$ ____	The Twelve Universal Laws	$18.95		$ ____
New Age Primer	$11.95		$ ____	**Ruth Ryden**				All My Angel Friends	$10.95		$ ____
Poisons That Heal	$14.95		$ ____	The Golden Path	$11.95		$ ____	Where Is God?	$ 6.95		$ ____
Prisoners of Earth	$11.95		$ ____	Living The Golden Path	$11.95		$ ____	Happy Feet	$ 6.95		$ ____
Sedona Vortex Guide Book	$14.95		$ ____	**Dorothy Roeder**				When the Earth Was New	$ 6.95		$ ____
Shadow of San Francisco Peaks	$ 9.95		$ ____	Crystal Co-Creators	$14.95		$ ____	The Angel Told Me ...	$ 6.95		$ ____
The Soul Remembers	$14.95		$ ____	Next Dimension is Love	$11.95		$ ____	Color Me One	$ 6.95		$ ____
Story of the People	$11.95		$ ____	Reach For Us	$14.95		$ ____	One Red Rose	$ 6.95		$ ____
This World and the Next One	$ 9.95		$ ____	**Hallie Deering**				Exploring the Chakras	$ 6.95		$ ____
Robert Shapiro/Arthur Fanning				Light From the Angels	$15.00		$ ____	Crystals For Kids	$ 6.95		$ ____
Shining the Light	$12.95		$ ____	Do-It-Yourself Power Tools	$25.00		$ ____	Who's Afraid of the Dark	$ 6.95		$ ____
Shining the Light — Book II	$14.95		$ ____	**Joshua David Stone, Ph.D.**				The Bridge Between Two Worlds	$ 6.95		$ ____
Shining the Light — Book III	$14.95		$ ____	Complete Ascension Manual	$14.95		$ ____				

BOOKS PRINTED OR MARKETED BY LIGHT TECHNOLOGY PUBLISHING

		No. Copies	Total			No. Copies	Total			No. Copies	Total
Access Your Brain's Joy Center	$14.95		$ ____	Spirit of The Ninja	$ 7.95		$ ____	**Barbara Marciniak**			
Awaken to the Healer Within	$16.50		$ ____	Temple of The Living Earth	$16.00		$ ____	Bringers of the Dawn	$12.95		$ ____
A Dedication to the Soul/Sole	$ 9.95		$ ____	The Only Planet of Choice	$14.95		$ ____	Earth	$12.95		$ ____
Earth in Ascension	$14.95		$ ____	The Pleiadian Agenda	$15.00		$ ____	**MSI**			
Galaxy Seven	$15.95		$ ____	The Transformative Vision	$14.95		$ ____	Ascension!	$11.95		$ ____
Innana Returns	$14.00		$ ____	Voices of Spirit	$13.00		$ ____	First Thunder	$12.95		$ ____
It's Time to Remember	$19.95		$ ____	We Are One	$14.95		$ ____	Second Thunder	$17.95		$ ____
I Want To Know	$ 7.00		$ ____	**Lee Carroll**				Enlightenment	$15.95		$ ____
Life Is The Father Within	$19.75		$ ____	Kryon—Book I, The End Times	$12.00		$ ____	**Preston B. Nichols with Peter Moon**			
Life On the Cutting Edge	$14.95		$ ____	Kryon—Book II, Don't Think Like .	$12.00		$ ____	Montauk Project	$15.95		$ ____
Look Within	$9.95		$ ____	Kryon—Book III, Alchemy of ...	$14.00		$ ____	Montauk Revisited	$19.95		$ ____
Mayan Calendar Birthday Book	$12.95		$ ____	Kryon—The Parables of Kryon	$17.00		$ ____	Pyramids of Montauk	$19.95		$ ____
Medical Astrology	$29.95		$ ____	**Richard Dannelley**				Encounter in the Pleiades ...	$19.95		$ ____
Our Cosmic Ancestors	$ 9.95		$ ____	Sedona Power Spot/Guide	$11.00		$ ____	**Lyssa Royal and Keith Priest**			
Out-Of-Body Exploration	$ 8.95		$ ____	Sedona: Beyond The Vortex	$12.00		$ ____	Preparing For Contact	$12.95		$ ____
Principles To Remember and Apply	$11.95		$ ____	**Tom Dongo: Mysteries of Sedona**				Prism of Lyra	$11.95		$ ____
Sedona Starseed	$14.95		$ ____	Mysteries of Sedona — Book I	$ 6.95		$ ____	Visitors From Within	$12.95		$ ____
Song of Sirius	$ 8.00		$ ____	Alien Tide — Book II	$ 7.95		$ ____	**Amorah Quan Yin**			
Soul Recovery and Extraction	$ 9.95		$ ____	Quest — Book III	$ 9.95		$ ____	The Pleiadian Workbook	$16.00		$ ____
				Unseen Beings, Unseen Worlds	$ 9.95		$ ____	Pleiadian Perspectives on ...	$14.00		$ ____
				Merging Dimensions	$14.95		$ ____				

ASCENSION MEDITATION TAPES

			No. Copies	Total				No. Copies	Total
Joshua David Stone, Ph.D.					Healing Meditations/Knowing Self	F102	$10.00		$ ____
Ascension Activation Meditation	S101	$12.00		$ ____	Manifestation & Alignment w/ Poles	F103	$10.00		$ ____
Tree of Life Ascension Meditation	S102	$12.00		$ ____	The Art of Shutting Up	F104	$10.00		$ ____
Mt. Shasta Ascension Activation Meditation	S103	$12.00		$ ____	Continuity of Consciousness	F105	$25.00		$ ____
Kabbalistic Ascension Activation	S104	$12.00		$ ____	Merging the Golden Light Replicas of You	F107	$10.00		$ ____
Complete Ascension Manual Meditation	S105	$12.00		$ ____	**Kryon/Lee Carroll**				
Set of all 5 tapes		$49.95		$ ____	Seven Responsibilities of the New Age	K101	$10.00		$ ____
Vywamus/Barbara Burns					Co-Creation in the New Age	K102	$10.00		$ ____
The Quantum Mechanical You (6 tapes)	B101-6	$40.00		$ ____	Ascension and the New Age	K103	$10.00		$ ____
Taka					Nine Ways to Raise the Planet's Vibration	K104	$10.00		$ ____
Magical Sedona through the Didgeridoo	T101	$12.00		$ ____	Gifts and Tools of the New Age	K105	$10.00		$ ____
Brian Grattan					**Jan Tober**				
Seattle Seminar Resurrection 1994 (12 tapes)	M102	$79.95		$ ____	Crystal Singer	J101	$12.00		$ ____
YHWH/Arthur Fanning									
On Becoming	F101	$10.00		$ ____					

Call, write or fax to request a complete catalog from Light Technology Publishing / Starchild Press!

☐ CHECK ☐ MONEY ORDER

CREDIT CARD: ☐ MC ☐ VISA

_____

Exp. date: _____

Signature: _____

(U.S. FUNDS ONLY) PAYABLE TO:

LIGHT TECHNOLOGY PUBLISHING

P.O. BOX 1526 • SEDONA • AZ 86339
(520) 282-6523 Fax: (520) 282-4130
1-800-450-0985
Fax 1-800-393-7017

BOOKSTORE DISCOUNTS HONORED — SHIPPING 15% OF RETAIL

NAME/COMPANY _____

ADDRESS _____

CITY/STATE/ZIP _____

PHONE _____ FAX _____

E-MAIL _____

SUBTOTAL: $ ____

SALES TAX: $ ____
(8.5% – AZ residents only)

SHIPPING/HANDLING: $ ____
($4 Min.; 15% of orders over '30)

CANADA S/H: $ ____
(20% of order)

TOTAL AMOUNT ENCLOSED: $ ____

All prices in US$. Higher in Canada and Europe. Books are available at all national distributors as well as the following international distributors:

CANADA: Dempsey (604) 683-5541 Fax (604) 683-5521 • ENGLAND/EUROPE: Windrush Press Ltd. 0608 652012/652025 Fax 0608 652125
AUSTRALIA: Gemcraft Books (03) 888-0111 Fax (03) 888-0044 • NEW ZEALAND: Peaceful Living Pub. (07) 571-8105 Fax (07) 571-8513